10 Rules Men Must Know in order to Deal with Women

by

Tariq "Elite" Nasheed

2010
G.D Publishing

King Flex Entertainment

10 Rules Men Must Know in order to Deal with Women

10 Rules Men Must Know in order to Deal with Women

ACKNOWLEDGMENTS

To all men who strive to reach Elite status in the game

TABLE OF CONTENTS

TABLE OF CONTENTS

INTRODUCTION

This book The Elite Way, is designed to give men straightforward rules about dating and relationships without the filter of political correctness. To some, the concept of rules as they pertain to relationships, may seem rigid, cold or calculating. After all, society has been taught that relationships are supposed to be based on spontaneity, chance encounters, luck and uncontrollable emotions. It's true that all potential relationships are somewhat of a gamble. But a good gambler has to know how to make educated bets.

Any game or situation you get into has to have rules for there to be order. If you play a game like blackjack or poker, it is gambling but it is still a game. It is a game of strategy. That's why poker is oftentimes considered a sport. And understanding and effectively dealing with women is a sport. That's why men who have mastered certain strategies to get women are oftentimes called "players."

So, what exactly is a sport? The definition of sport is any activity that is governed by a set of rules or customs that are often engaged in competitively. So, dealing with women is no longer a gamble; it should be considered a sport. In any sport, you have to train, you have to have discipline and you have to think strategically. Now, you don't have to be a player, per se, in order to implement certain strategies for dealing with women. But to be thorough, you have to abide by a certain set of rules. These rules can be ones that were taught to you or they can be self-imposed.

When you have self-imposed rules, this is called integrity, and integrity is the soul of the game. Integrity keeps you grounded. Integrity is when you have rules for yourself that you will not compromise.

The Importance of Having a Soul Within Your Game

According to popular folklore and mythology, anything without a soul is lifeless. If you don't have a soul,so the myth goes, you become a zombie or a vampire. What is a vampire? A vampire is a soulless, half-dead creature that preys on the living. And this is what happens to people without a soul who get into the dating game with no rules or integrity to keep them grounded. They become parasites or scavengers. They have no rules or standards. They try to leach off others and in many ways, they emotionally victimize people they date. When you have no standards, you will allow yourself to dip into the bottom of the barrel of the dating pool. You will date lackluster women, you will reduce yourself to paying for sex on a regular basis, you will tolerate disrespectful and humiliating behavior,etc. And this will slowly chip away at your self-esteem. Some men will consciously try to rationalize this bottom of the barrel type dating by coming up with slogans like "It ain't trickin' if you got it," or referring to overweight women they date as "thick." But subconsciously, they know they would like to do better. The purpose of this book is to help you make better relationship decisions based on your fullest potential.

THE FORMULA

Not only will this book teach you about the rules of dating and relationships, you will also learn the formula for dealing with women. I call this formula GIC^2. This formula is based on the three essential elements a man needs in order to consistently be successful at dealing with women.

1. **Game**

   A procedure or strategy for gaining a result; also the set of rules governing the sport of dealing with women

2. **Intelligence**

   The ability to understand complex ideas, to adapt to certain environments and to learn from experience.

3. **Common Sense**

   Sound, practical judgment.

When a number or equation is squared, that means it is multiplied times itself. So, when you multiply the GIC formula times itself, meaning practice it consistently, your skills become *infinite*, and your game will reach ELITE status. For each of the ten rules I discuss in this book, I will explain which equation in the GIC^2 formula best applies to it.

The Three Stages of Dating

This book is broken down into three basic stages that pertain to dating and relationships.

1.**The Campaign Stage**

This is when men are out in the field looking for women to date. The first three rules of this book will teach men the best ways to get their foot in the door with women.

2.**The Maintenance Stage**

This is when men are actually in relationships. Many men don't understand that meeting and campaigning for women is only half the challenge. The process of actually maintaining a relationship brings on a whole new set of challenges that are not often discussed when it comes to techniques in dating. Rules numbers 4-7 will address ways to help men maintain their manhood, integrity and peace of mind in relationships.

3.**The Recovery Stage**

No matter how optimistic we are about getting into new relationships, the reality is some relationships simply don't work out. Rules 8-10 will help give you insight on how to get over a severed relationship, how to regroup and get your mind right and how to move forward to a new situation.

Now remember, in order for all of these strategies, formulas and techniques laid out in this book to work effectively, you have to be grounded in integrity. If you want to use the information in this book to try to just get over on people, this might work temporarily, but it will not give you any positive, long-term results. Using this book without integrity just makes you a scam artist, and most scams depend purely on luck. The problem with that is luck runs out. But you can always keep using strategies.

Having integrity in your game does not mean you have to be Mr. Nice Guy all the time. Having integrity allows you to be fair when dealing with women in relationships. There's a time to be nice and there's a time to be stern. The rules in this book will help you find that balance. Once you have mastered these rules and implemented them within the rolodex of your subconscious mind, there is only one way you will handle dating and relationships from that point on – the Elite Way.

SECTION I

THE CAMPAIGN STAGE

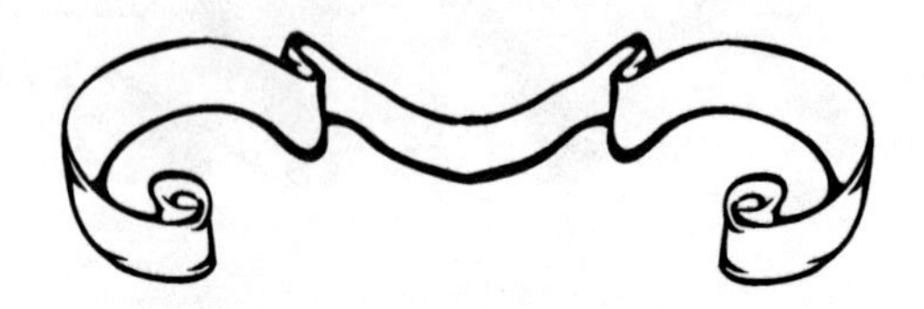

WHEN THERE IS NO ENEMY WITHIN, THE ENEMIES OUTSIDE CANNOT HURT YOU.
— AFRICAN PROVERB

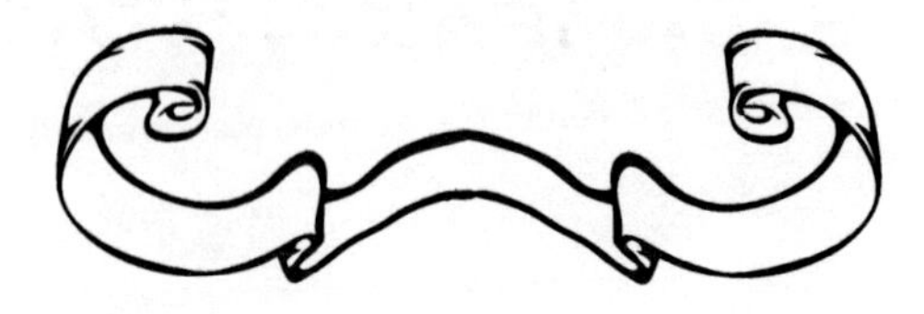

RULE 1

GET CONFIDENCE FROM WITHIN

To be effective at campaigning for females, you have to have the foundation of confidence. As a matter of fact, to be truly effective at anything, be it good or bad, you have to have some type of confidence in what you're doing. You can't even be an effective criminal without having a certain level of confidence, (not that I'm advocating anyone becoming a criminal). The term "con man" is a shortened version of the phrase "confidence man." In the mid-1800s, confidence men were scam artists and swindlers who would approach random people and hustle them out of their money, jewelry and other valuables by gaining their confidence. So whatever you're trying to attain from another person, you have to get people confident in you. In the case of getting women, you're trying to attain cooperation. But in order to attain that cooperation, you have to be confident in yourself.

Gaining Self-Confidence

Whenever the subject of gaining confidence is discussed, we usually receive the same old cliché advice that states that you should "feel good about yourself" or "you have to believe to achieve", etc. People like to say how much you need to have confidence, but people rarely go in-depth on how you get that confidence. Confidence is more than feeling good about yourself. Some people feel good about themselves based on superficial achievements. Some people can get drunk or high and feel good about themselves. Some people can rent an expensive car or get expensive clothes and feel good about themselves. But these things only give you a false sense of confidence because they are all based on external things. Real confidence comes from within. You can lose external things or they can be taken away from you. But the level of confidence you draw from within you can never be taken away because it's something that you control.

Getting the Winner's Vibe

Let's face it – for many people, confidence is about winning. At the end of the day, you want to feel like a winner.

And feeling like a winner will make you more attractive to females. One way to get real confidence from within is to get that winner's vibe. In order to win at anything, you have to play the game. Like the old saying goes, "You have to be in it to win it." Even if you feel that the odds are stacked against you, you still have to put your bid in, so to speak. In order to win, you have to take risks. In order to take risks, you have to *try*. Many people don't win, not because they are losers but because they are quitters. In many cases, when certain guys go to clubs and social settings to meet women and they get any kind of minor apprehension from a female, they're ready to throw in the towel and go home.

The two easiest things to be in life is a quitter and a hater. A quitter is a person who gives up too easily because of a lack of confidence. A hater is a person who gives up too easily and who tries to project their lack of confidence and self-doubt onto others. So you never want to fall into the hater's trap because eventually that mentality will create a loser's vibe within you. You will find fault with other people because you no longer have a desire to win. If you want to reject the loser's vibe and acquire a winner's vibe, you have to eliminate any fear you have about taking a risk.

Trusting Yourself

A major facet of gaining real confidence is trusting yourself. We have confidence in certain people in our lives because we trust them. We trust our doctors, we trust our teachers. We trust our local politicians, we trust our judges. We have confidence in these people and we trust them because we assume they know about what they're doing. We assume that they're experts in their field of work. We trust them and have confidence in them because we feel that they're knowledgeable in their chosen occupations. So, if you want to have real self-confidence, you need to apply that same level of trust to *yourself.*

Many guys don't trust themselves when they have the opportunity to step to women. They feel that they are not going to make a good impression. They feel like they are going to say the wrong thing. They feel like they might get dissed. And having an internal fear of all these things will show in your attitude, your body language and your demeanor, making you appear less confident. But if you trust yourself, and know that you have integrity , that you're going to be yourself ,and that you are going to try to do your best no matter what the outcome is, you will have mastered one of the secrets of real self-confidence.

Knowledge + Game = Real Self Confidence

Confidence is also about the accumulation of knowledge. The more information you have, the more game you have. The more you know, the more you flow. Information translates into intelligence. As a matter of fact, when the military is trying to get information about a potential opponent, they call it "gathering intelligence". The more information, knowledge and intelligence you have about a vast array of subjects, the more self trust you will have. You will have this self trust because you will feel like you know what you're talking about.

Also, when you step to women, you won't feel the anxiety of being at a loss for words because increasing your level of knowledge and intelligence automatically increases your vocabulary. And when a man is having a conversation with a female and he has the ability to give the right verbal responses and say the right thing at the right time without missing a beat, this comes off as a major sign of confidence.

False Confidence versus Real Confidence

As I noted before, some people gain a false sense of confidence based on superficial or external things. Some men feel confident after they luck up and get some play from an attractive female. Some people feel confident after they go shopping or get a new haircut. While these things should make you feel like you are on top of your game, your level of confidence should never be based on these things. When your level of confidence is based on behavior such as displaying name brand clothes, rocking the latest jewelry, or rolling around in luxury cars, this makes you look flashy. And being flashy oftentimes makes you look insecure.

If you notice, many wealthy men are not flashy. There are men who are millionaires who dress so casual and low-key you would never think that they had money. Many rich people do not get confidence from material things. Their confidence is based on their **knowledge**. They are aware that they have the knowledge and the game to accumulate material things. Having that level of confidence helps you relax around women and be yourself.

Whenever you give off the appearance of trying to impress women, this makes you look somewhat weak and unsure of yourself. But when you appear to be comfortable in your own skin, this displays an inner confidence that women are attracted to. Now, the first step to getting real confidence is acknowledging if you are displaying behavior that reflects false confidence. The following list will desplay a few behavior patterns of a person with false confidence and the behavior patterns of a person with real confidence.

You have false confidence:

when you feel threatened by others

when you are loud and obnoxious

when you bully people

when you constantly brag about yourself

when you excessively display material items

Real confidence is:

when you can congratulate others

when you are calm and self-assured

when you can show respect and gratitude

when you can try to remain somewhat of a mystery

when you are comfortable with your knowledge to accumulate material things

If you notice, the characteristics of a person with false confidence involve them overtly trying to bring attention to themselves. And the characteristics of a person with real confidence involve them deflecting attention *away* from themselves and putting the spotlight on others. So, when you're socializing with women and you're trying to blatantly bring attention to yourself, you will usually receive the opposite results. Many men will gravitate towards women who are attention hounds. But women usually are put off by men who are attention hounds because this type of attention in a man reeks of insecurity. Women usually go for the strong, silent type. By silent, I don't mean standing around like a monk not making a sound. I mean being silent about yourself, not bragging about yourself and not trying to bring superficial attention to yourself. By taking the spotlight off yourself and placing it onto the female you are talking to, this shows you are confident with yourself. And when a female sees that you're confident with yourself, she will be confident with you, too.

How to Build Your Confidence

One of the best ways to help build up your confidence is to set goals no matter how big or small for yourself. As I stated before, confidence is about winning, and winning is about achieving. So, you want to get into the habit of achieving things on a regular basis. This way it won't seem so far-fetched to achieve cooperation from females. By setting goals you will get into the cycle of planning, action, and achievement. This way, you won't depend on luck when dealing with women. You will be used to depending on strategy. Here's a confidence building exercise you should start doing immediately. You can start doing this technique for one week. After the first week, you can continue at your own pace.

Every day for one week, you should set five small goals or errands for yourself. It could be something as simple as going to the mall, mowing your lawn, going to the gym, etc. You can even set bigger goals if you like. Whatever goal you set, make sure you stick with it no matter what. When you set a goal and you stick to it, you learn how to become a man of your word. And when you are a man of your word, you build integrity and you learn to trust yourself. And when you trust yourself, you will be confident in yourself.

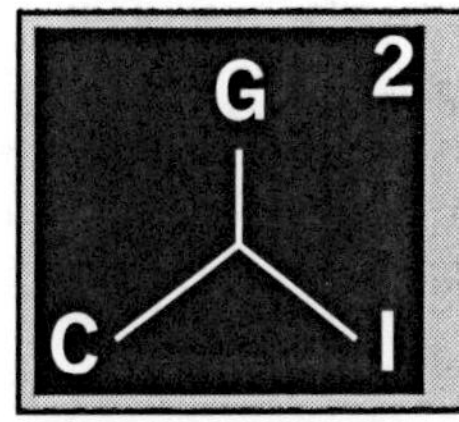

Rule One applies to the element of GAME because it will help you build character, integrity, and standards for yourself

5 Best Places to Campaign for Females

1. **Bookstores**
2. **Gyms/Fitness Clubs**
3. **Restaurants**
4. **Charity Events**
5. **Health Food Stores**

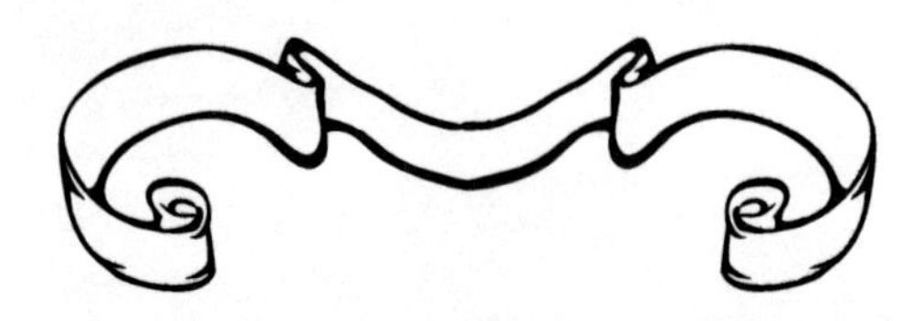

TO SPEAK AND TO SPEAK WELL
ARE TWO THINGS. A FOOL MAY TALK,
BUT A WISE MAN SPEAKS.
— BEN JONSON

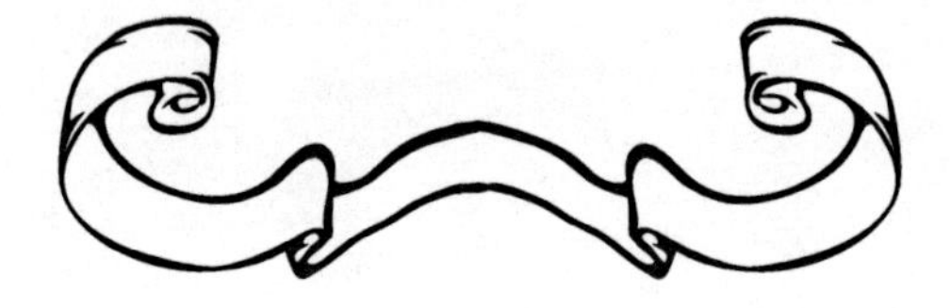

RULE 2

EXERCISING YOUR GAME MUSCLE

When people have been out of the dating scene for a while (or if they have never been in the dating scene at all), they oftentimes make reference to their game being rusty. When anything sits idle for a period of time, it gets weak, eroded or rusty. If a car is parked and has not been driven in a long time, the battery will die and it will need a charge. If a weapon such as a handgun has not been fired or properly maintained, it has the potential to jam up when you try to use it. If you are a physically fit person who stopped lifting weights for a long period of time, eventually your muscles will weaken. And when you get back into the gym, your muscles will get stiff, sore and uncomfortable from working out. Well, the same thing happens to your game muscle when it's not being utilized on a regular basis. Your game will get weak, your conversation will jam up on you, and you will need to recharge or reenergize your game. Your game muscle is your mouthpiece and your mouthpiece is your conversation.

The Importance of Verbal Game

I always get emails from men asking me how to meet women off social networking sites such as Facebook, Myspace, Twitter, etc. Now, these are excellent mediums to socialize with women, but it's somewhat of a gift and a curse. The gift is that the technology allows you to interact and share information instantly with a wide range of people. The curse is that these sites do not give men a chance to exercise their game muscle.

When you are typing and texting back and forth, you don't get to effectively verbalize and get across your feelings and emotions. Ironically, by constantly utilizing these social networking sites without making any real world connections, this will eventually make you more anti-social. Back in the day before social networking sites (and before the Internet), men had no choice but to use their game muscle when dealing with women. If a man liked a female, there was no Myspace, no Facebook, no text messaging or cell phones for him to use to communicate back and forth with her . So, if a guy was interested in a girl, he would have to iron his clothes, get himself groomed and go over to the young ladies' house and *talk* to her.

The Lost Art of Talking

The rise of online social networking sites, email and text messaging has delivered a prominent blow to the art of talking. As I stated before, the technology is great but it has made many of us lazy when it comes to campaigning for females. Many people have become dependent upon texting and online chatting. Before this technology, you would have to make yourself presentable and you had to be capable of holding a decent verbal conversation. You also had to be able to communicate non-verbally and get your point across by use of your voice inflections, emotions and body language. Society has now become so dependent upon this technology, that people have to actually text their emotions to one another by using terms like LOL (laughing out loud), SMH (shaking my head) and smiley faces and frowning faces, etc. It's gotten to the point where some people will go out on an actual physical date, and instead of talking with each other, they will sit there texting away on their two-ways or their Blackberry phones.

The point is, because of certain technology, the dating game has evolved and has now been designed to focus less and less on verbal conversations. So, the result is the game muscle of many men has become weakened. And many guys simply don't know how to effectively conduct a decent conversation with females. Notice I said *effectively* conduct a decent conversation because there are some guys who will step to women and they will talk their ears off. But if you're not having an effective conversation and getting positive responses and cooperation from females, then the words are pointless.

Pitfalls to Avoid

In today's culture, styles usually change every six months, and if you've been out of the loop for a significant period of time, it's easy for your game to get outdated when you try to step back into the arena. This is a major fear that many guys have when they're getting back into the dating scene. They wonder if a female would still be interested in them if they're not up on the latest trends, lingo and fashion. Well, the good news is you really don't have to worry about all that.

When you're back into the dating game campaigning for females, just be yourself. Just be relaxed and just chill. Being chill never goes out of style. Even the term "chill" has been around for decades. When you are yourself and you remain chill, you don't feel the nervous pressure of having to win people over. Now, when you jump back on the campaign trail and you're trying to get the rust off your game, try not to fall into these three main pitfalls that many men experience:

1. **Don't confide in women**

A lot of men who've been out of the dating scene for a while will meet new females and make the mistake of turning the interaction into a therapy session. The harsh reality is when most women are going out, especially when they're out to have a good time, the last thing they want to do is listen to some random guy's problems. Keep your problems to yourself and keep yourself a mystery. This way, women will project their desires onto you.

2. **Don't Gossip**

A lot of times, when men are in social spots and they are getting some cooperation from a woman, they tend to run out of things to say. The key to mastering the art of the game is to control the flow of the conversation. You don't control the flow of the conversation by talking a lot. You do it by saying the right things and asking the right questions. Controlling the flow of the conversation makes you look more confident because you subconsciously and subliminally put the other person in a position of trying to gain your approval. It's as if you're interviewing them to see if they're worthy of your attention. When guys lose control of the flow of the conversation, the female takes over and the guy usually follows her lead. And in many cases, this leads men to gossiping with women. This is a major no-no. Sitting around with women talking about what celebs are dating who and what you heard about this person or that person is not a good look for a guy. As a man, you never want to seem petty. You have to always appear to be above that type of conversation.

3.**Don't cupcake with women you just met**

The definition of "cupcaking" is: [**kuhp**-keyk-ing] verb– *the act of being overly affectionate or complimentary to a person you desire.* In many cases, when a guy gets back into the dating field and his game is a little rusty, he will make the mistake of being too complimentary to females. By constantly giving women praise, you're putting yourself in a position of weakness and subservience.

When you're trying to cuddle and cupcake with women when you first meet them, this gives off an aura of desperation. By giving women unwarrented praises, you are deferring to them in a sense. And women are not generally attracted to men that they can have control over so easily. Now, if you are in a committed relationship with a woman, a little cupcaking is understandable because then the woman is in a position to earn that type of attention and affection from you. But you never cupcake with a female you just met.

Shake Off Anti-Social Energy

Another thing that happens when you've been out of the dating scene for a while is the accumulation of anti-social energy. This happens because many men lose track of how to effectively socialize. This is based generally on a lack of confidence and other fears. This type of behavior creates negative tension and unwarranted assumptions about the opposite sex. Have you ever been in a situation where you were out and you saw a female that you were interested in but you didn't step to her? In many cases, when men don't approach the female of their desire, they automatically begin assuming the worst. They say things like, "she looks stuck up," or "she looks like she's mean." Men do this because they're projecting their own anti-social energy onto the female. In most cases when you actually talk to these females, they're usually more down to earth than you assumed. So always shake off these negative thoughts and energy that tend to creep up in your mind when you are campaigning for females.

How to Exercise Your Game Muscle

No matter how good you are at a something, you should always practice at it. No matter what type of talent or skill you have, you should always go through exercises to tweak, tighten and expand your range or level of strength. When a person goes to the gym and starts working out, after a while they become muscular. After they become muscular, they just can't stop working out because they reached their goal. They have to keep exercising to maintain their stature.

Every now and then, a major A-list Hollywood actor will appear in a small, Broadway play production. A few years ago, Oscar award winner Julia Roberts starred in a play called *Three Days of Rain*, and two-time Oscar award winning actor, Denzel Washington, starred in a Broadway play called *Julius Caesar*. Now both of these movie stars make around 20 million dollars a film each. So, they didn't need to do stage plays for financial or career reasons. They did these stage productions because they respected their craft and they wanted to exercise their acting chops. I'm assuming their logic is, when you're on a big budget film set in this day and age, many times you don't get to expand your range as a true actor.

Movie actors, nowadays, have CGI for their movies, they have stunt doubles, they have stand-ins, they get to do different takes from different angles. They have luxurious catering services. They have assistants attending to their every need on set. And because of this, many actors will begin to lose their edge because they've become too relaxed and complacent within their craft. But live stage acting is considered the purest form of acting because everything from beginning to end is in the moment. When you are on stage in front of a live audience there's no CGI to depend on, there are no stops, there are no double takes from different angles, there are no stunt doubles, there is no editing. You can't depend on anything but your acting skills. And when these things are being utilized every night in front of a live audience, it makes your game more focused. It makes you more spontaneous, and it makes your game tighter. And this same mentality can be applied to you trying to exercise your game muscle in order for you to step to women correctly.

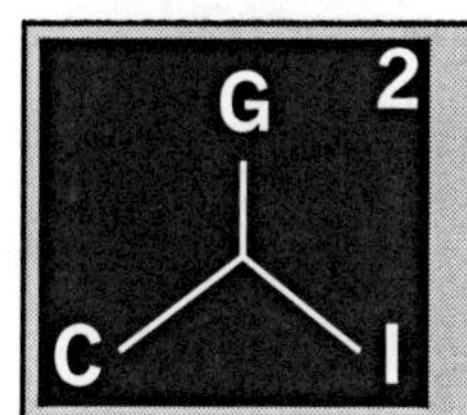

Rule Two applies to the element of GAME because it teaches you how to strengthen your verbal skills to get the results you want

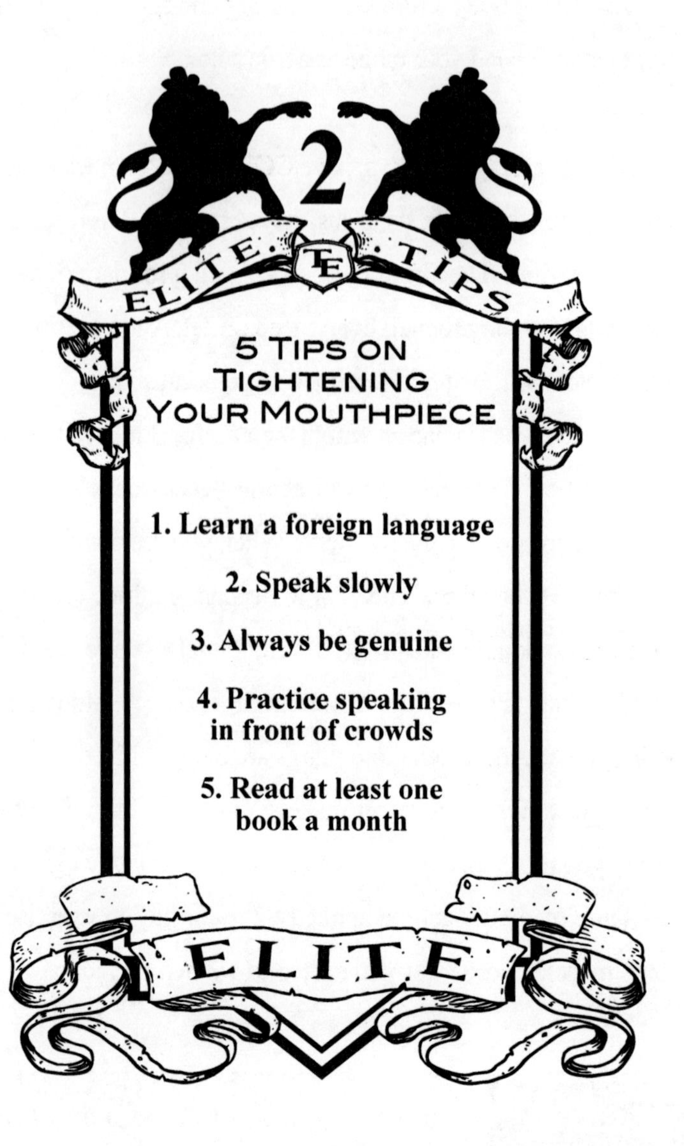

5 Tips on Tightening Your Mouthpiece

1. Learn a foreign language

2. Speak slowly

3. Always be genuine

4. Practice speaking in front of crowds

5. Read at least one book a month

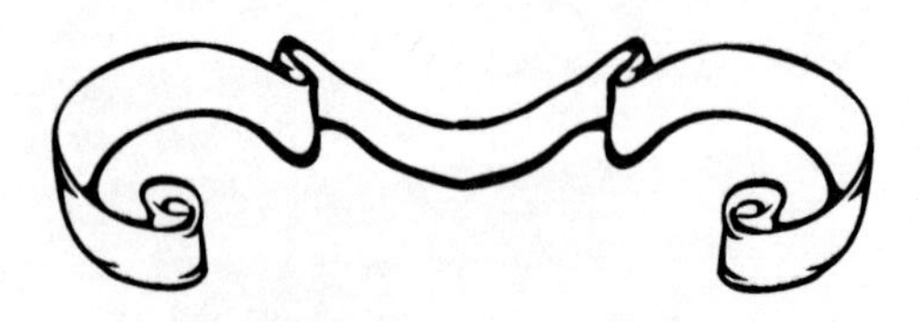

THE WORLD IS A BOOK,
AND THOSE WHO DO NOT TRAVEL
READ ONLY A PAGE.
— ST. AUGUSTINE

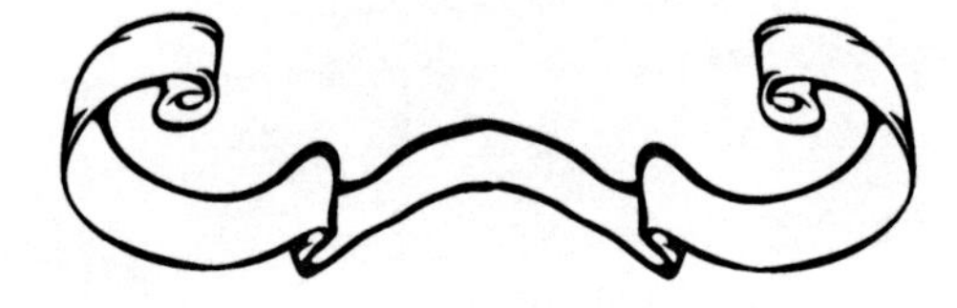

RULE 3

DON'T CONFINE YOURSELF

The reason many men get limited results when they are campaigning for women is because they often limit their horizons. Just like a good politician, when you're trying to get elected, you can't stay in one district. You have to hit the campaign trail and expose yourself to new voters, so to speak. So, this same dynamic applies to campaigning for women. Many people like to remain in a safety zone. They're comfortable remaining in one area where they're familiar with the people and their surroundings. Now this mentality is cool if you are in a committed relationship or if you're trying to settle down, but if you're in the campaign stage, it is imperative that you do not confine yourself to one specific geographical location.

Removing Limitations

Before you can go beyond your geographical locations, you have to remove any mental limitations you may have. Many people don't see or visualize beyond their immediate perspective. This is because many people have an innate fear of failure. So, in their minds, it's easier to stay in a safety zone mentally and physically than to cope with the thought of failing. A lot of guys will stay in the same city they grew up in and deal with the same types of women that particular city has to offer year in and year out. And if the level of cooperation and quality of these women is subpar, these men will just make the best out of a bad situation.

Many of these men live by the old adage, "If life gives you lemons, you might as well make lemonade." Well, I say, if life gives you lemons, don't make lemonade, go someplace where there is better fruit. When you stay in one spot and settle for lemons, you begin to lower your standards in general. You have to realize that there is a big world out there. Everything doesn't revolve around the 20-mile radius in which you live. In the outside world there are billions of other women out there who are potentially compatible with you. So remove your mental limitations during the campaign stage by realizing that you do not have to settle for the women or the lifestyle in your immediate vicinity if you're not completely satisfied with them. This dynamic can be applied to other aspects of your life as well.

For example, when I was putting together my men's cologne line, *Risqué Elite*, I first began looking for manufacturers where I lived in the Los Angeles area. And when I couldn't the results I wanted, my assistants and I began looking for manufacturers all along the West Coast. When that didn't work, we began to contact companies on the East Coast and the Midwest. We found a few companies in New York that had the quality we wanted, but they were trying to charge ridiculous prices. So, we contacted a few companies in the Southern states. We found a company in Florida that had better prices, but I wasn't 100% satisfied with the quality of their bottles and labeling. So, instead of trying to compromise my standards and settle for what was readily available here in the States, I decided to look for companies overseas. We contacted companies in China, India and Italy, and we finally found an excellent manufacturer in France that gave us the quality and the pricing that exceeded our expectations. And I was 110% satisfied with the finished product.

This same dynamic is applicable when you are dealing with women. If you have a limited mindset, you will compromise your standards and make concessions with halfway decent and in some cases not so decent women because you feel you can't do any better. So remove your mental limitations during the campaign stage by realizing that you do not have to settle for the women and the lifestyle in your immediate vicinity

Self-Imposed Solitary Confinement

Oftentimes, when you get into a pattern of limiting yourself, you unwittingly place yourself into a state of self-imposed solitary confinement, and there are many detrimental ramifications when doing this. The concept of solitary confinement has been historically used for torture, punishment or protection. In the prison system, in order to punish an inmate, he's placed in solitary confinement. This technique is done oftentimes to break the inmate down mentally. As humans, our minds are charged with energy and that energy has to be exerted outwardly. This is one of the reasons why we have a social structure. People have an instinctive drive to socialize and connect with other people. Once we're placed into a situation of extended confinement, either self-imposed or forced upon us, the energy in our minds gets backed up because it is not being released. And all that built up energy can cause you to go insane. This is why people who have been placed in situations of solitary confinement often complain of having hallucinations, they complain of having voices in their heads and they complain of having other psychological disorders.

Even though these are extreme examples, the same things happen to a person who confines themselves to a certain location all their lives. Some people stay stressed. Some people might stay on edge.Some people might get feelings of depressions. And some people might build up nervous anxiety, and every minor thing in their lives becomes magnified and overly dramatic because they have an unfulfilled need for adventure.

As I stated before, another reason some people place themselves in solitary confinement is because of protection. In prison, some inmates just can't cut it in the general population. In many cases, when an inmate is under the threat of being physically harmed, he asks to be placed in PC (protective custody), which is basically solitary confinement. Many men in the outside world place themselves in this same protective custody within their homes and neighborhoods because they fear they cannot cut it in the rest of the world. They have a classic fear of the unknown. They also have a fear of rejection from women and other aspects of life outside of their familiar realm.

The Neutral Mind State

When you confine yourself to a familiar location in order to feel a sense of psychological or emotional protection you will often create a neutral mind state. You will feel safe and you will feel comfortable, but you will not grow mentally. And being too comfortable to the point that you remain in a neutral mind state is not always good for you. When a car is running in neutral, it doesn't go forward, it doesn't go in reverse – it just stays in one spot. And even though the car will be safe from the dangers of the road, so to speak, it will eventually run out of gas and stop functioning. It will burn a significant amount of fuel and energy without ever going anywhere. The way you utilize your game works the same way. You burn the same amount of energy sitting in a neutral zone within your familiar surroundings as you would exploring the world and putting yourself in a position to accomplish different things. This includes interacting with a better selection of women.

Don't Be a Cyber-Player

Now some guys might read this information about campaigning for women in different areas and say to themselves, "Well, this is easy. I'll just chat online with women from different cities." Now this technique is good for introduction purposes, but you still have to take your game on the road. You don't want to end up being a cyber-player. A cyber-player is a guy who stays on his computer getting into chat-room and e-mail relationships with random screen names. Notice I said screen names instead of females. Because in many cases,you don't know who is behind some of these screen names. It could be a female,or it could be a man pretending to be a female.The point is, unless you are interacting with a person face-to-face, in the flesh, it is not a real relationship.

Hitting the Road

In order to campaign effectively and have real relationships with a diverse group of women, you have to physically hit the road. You do not need to travel across the country or around the world (though the more you travel, the better your odds to meet women you are compatible with). Going to different parts of your own city that you've never been to will suffice. If you live in a midtown area and you feel like you've exhausted all of your resources in your local dating pool, you should go to social spots on the outskirts or the suburbs of your town, and vice versa. If you live in the suburbs, start hitting up some midtown spots. If you want to expand your campaign a little, start hitting up the next biggest city close to yours on the weekends. If the game isn't working for you in one city, you will definitely find your groove in another town. Different cities have different collective mindsets. In some cities, the people are generally more energetic. In other cities, the people might be a little more conservative. This is a good thing because all of our personalities are different, and you might receive a different level of cooperation from females depending on which city best fits your vibe.

Getting Reference Points

Traveling and taking your game on the road also teaches you how to interact and tailor your game to different types of women. Just knowing the different types of personalities that individual women have in other parts of the country and other parts of the world will give you reference points. This is very important because, the problem that many men have when it comes to interacting with women, is that they are used to dealing with only one type of woman. The only reference points these men have are the women they grew up with.

For example, if a guy grew up around only rural area females or "country" girls, when he encounters a "city" girl, his game might fall flat. This is because he doesn't have a mental reference on how to engage a city girl. Let's say you're a guy who grew up in a major metropolitan area, and you're used to dealing with the fast-paced females of the big city. If you interacted with a small-town girl for the first time, your game might go over her head. So, it's important to travel and learn about the different cultures and personalities that many women have based on their geographic locations. This way you can have a head start on tailoring your game when you're on a serious campaign trail.

Creating a Mysterious Effect

Another good thing about taking your game on the road is that being in other cities gives you the appearance of being mysterious. Women have always been intrigued by men with a mysterious vibe. And the females in your town or community who you grew up around, they already know you or they know someone who knows you, and they are used to seeing you. And people are generally not intrigued by things that they are used to. But in another city nobody knows who you are and nobody knows your vibe. And you can use this to your advantage.

When you go to different cities, let the females project their own desires and fantasies onto you. Try to remain as mysterious as possible. You don't have to be deceptive or disingenuous with these females that you meet. Just keep information about yourself at a minimum and watch the game work wonders for you.

Traveling on a Budget

Now, I know a lot of you might be thinking, "Isn't all of this traveling somewhat expensive?" Contrary to popular belief, it's really not as expensive to travel as people think. And to be quite frank, I believe a lot of people like to use the "traveling is too expensive" excuse as a cop-out. Like I said before, many of these people are just afraid of the thought of failure, and many of them have a fear of change. In reality, you can go online at any given time and find reasonable deals on all-inclusive trips to Las Vegas, Miami, New York, Hollywood, Hawaii, etc. So, the opportunity is out there. You just have to want to do it.

If some of these guys simply stopped paying their "trick tabs" and "cupcaking bills" ("making it rain" in strip clubs and spending most of their paychecks on dates with un-cooperative females), they would have the means to travel. You should also understand that there is a difference between vacationing and traveling. Vacationing can seem somewhat expensive because generally,this is when people go out of town and engage in leisurely activities. But if you simply want to travel,you can pack up a bag or throw on a back pack, and just hit the road if you so desire.

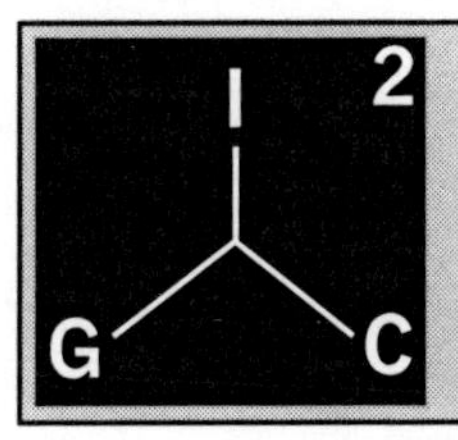

Rule Three applies to the element of INTELLIGENCE because it encourages you to explore the world and gather information globally

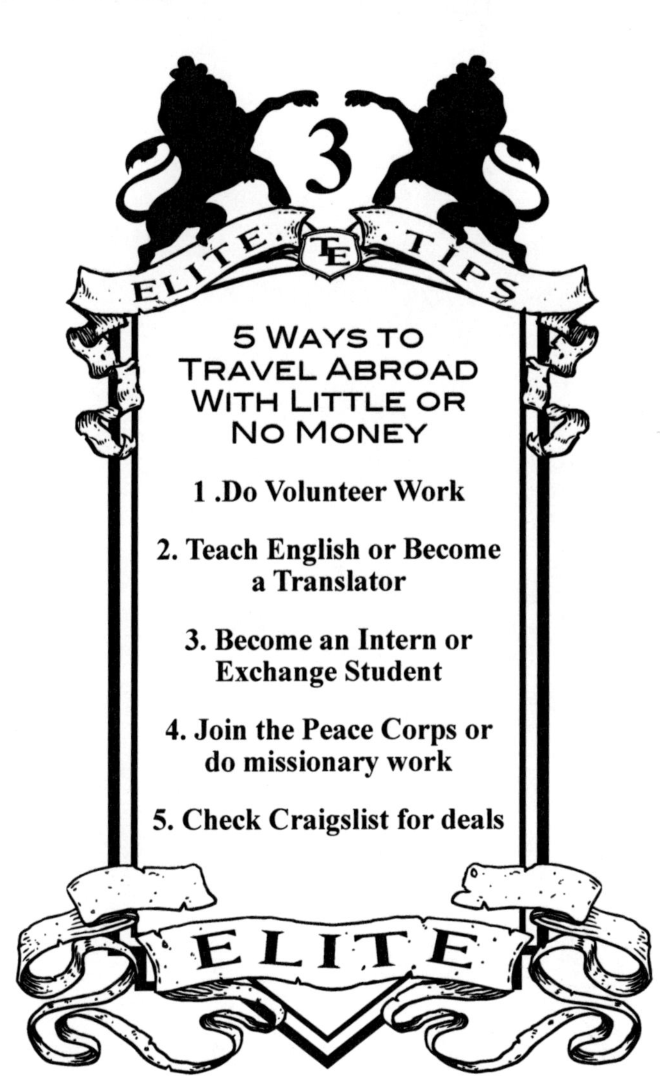

Section II

The Maintenance Stage

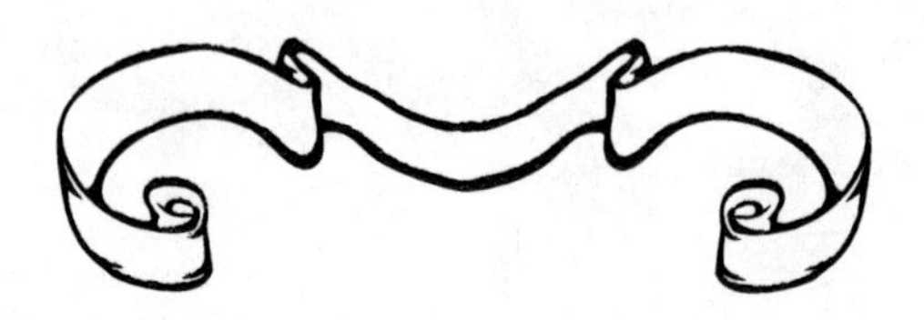

WHEN YOU ARE THROUGH
CHANGING,
YOU ARE THROUGH.
— BRUCE BARTON

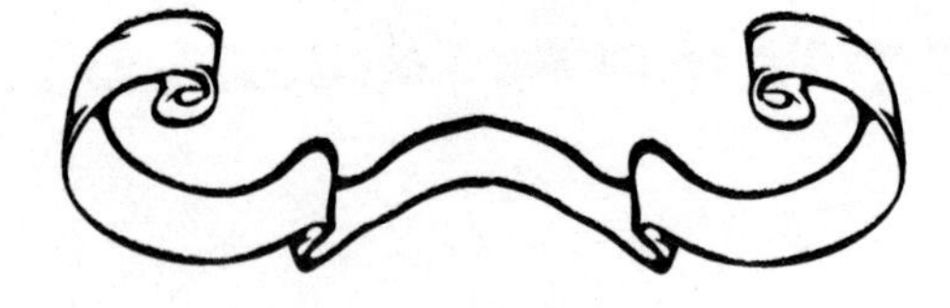

RULE 4

HAVE A JEKYLL AND HYDE MENTALITY

Now that you have an understanding of what it takes to have a successful campaign, it's now time to explore how to maintain your game once you are in a committed relationship. The first thing you need to learn is the importance of having a Jekyll and Hyde mentality. The term "Jekyll and Hyde" stems from the popular 19th century novella *Strange Case of Dr. Jekyll and Mr. Hyde*. This is a story about a mild-mannered doctor who drinks a liquid potion that he concocted and takes on an evil split personality. Now as far as you having a Jekyll and Hyde mentality when it comes to maintaining your relationships, this doesn't mean you have to take on an evil or violent persona. This simply means that sometimes you have to show different sides of your personality, even if that personality isn't considered politically correct, so to speak.

The Balance of Good and Evil

In many cases, for an entity, including relationships, to be successful or effective, there has to be a balance of good and evil. This dynamic can be seen in many parts of our own culture. In cases, for example, where law enforcement is trying to effectively interrogate a suspect, they use the classic "good cop/bad cop" routine in order to gain a confession. This dynamic can also be seen in politics. When ex-president George W. Bush was in office, he was portrayed as the simple, good old boy, whereas his vice-president, Dick Cheney, was known for being hard-lined and stern. In the Obama campaign for the presidency, Vice-presidential candidate, Joe Biden, was considered a "bulldog" behind the scenes while presidential candidate Obama was the charismatic front man.

This dynamic can also be seen in the entertainment and business world as well. Many influential and successful rap music labels were known for having charismatic front men – the good guys – with the hardass, no-nonsense businessmen in the background – the bad guys. Ruthless Records had the late rapper, Easy-E, as the charismatic front man and the notoriously no-nonsense businessman, Jerry Heller was running things from the shadows. The infamous Death Row Records had Dr. Dre as the likeable front man, while the notorious hardcore

Suge Knight ran things from behind the scenes. The rap label Rocafella Records had rapper Jay Z as the likeable, charismatic, good guy in the forefront, with the designated bad guy, (by his own admission) Damon Dash, handling business behind the scenes. In the early stages of the greatest rap label ever, Def Jam, Russell Simmons was the charismatic front man, with the rigid, no nonsense business partner by the name of Lyor Cohen calling the shots from the background.

The point is, the balance of good and evil, the good guy/bad guy scenario, is very important in order to have an effective relationship. And in the case of dating and relationships, you have to play the dual roles yourself. If you lean too much on the good guy side, people might take your goodness for weakness and try to run over you. And you are too much of a bad guy, this will repel too many people away from you. So the key to the game is to learn how to delicately balance the two scenarios.

Put Some Yang in Your Game

In ancient Chinese culture there's a philosophy that states, everything in nature has opposites called the Yin and the Yang. This philosophy states, without one the other would not exist.

Without hot there would be no cold. Without day there would be no night. Without pain there would be no pleasure, and so on. Another part of this philosophy states that Yin represents the feminine, passive side and the Yang represents the masculine opposite. In today's culture, men are constantly being influenced to get in touch with their feminine side. This often leads to a lot of passivity in men when it comes to relationships.

Passivity is generally a feminine characteristic. And too much feminine energy coming from the woman and man in the relationship causes an imbalance. And if there is a general imbalance in the relationship, it will eventually dissolve. This is why men need to start putting some more Yang in the Game.

As a man, don't be afraid to show your masculine side. Don't be afraid to give off masculine energy. Playing the passive, nice guy role, constantly trying to appease and win brownie points with your female mate will further suppress your true feelings. And eventually you might end up acting out in passive aggressive ways; by lying, by having secret affairs outside of the relationships, by using backhanded compliments to insult your mate, exhibiting rebellious behavior, etc.

It is very unhealthy to suppress your true feelings in

relationships. Many experts agree that the root of all problems in relationships is basically the lack of proper communication. So, you should always man up and communicate how you really feel about certain situations in your relationships, even if you risk coming across as a jerk or an A-hole.

Don't Be Afraid To Be a Dick

Oftentimes, when a man is considered rude, stern or uncompromising, a certain slang term is applied to him. And what is interesting is this is the same slang word for the most basic representation of masculinity in the male form – the male genitalia: The Dick.

The term dick is usually applied in a derogatory context to an authoritative figure with an unrelenting, dispassionate demeanor. You will often hear people say things like, "I wanted to get some days off from work, but my boss was being a dick." Or they will say, "I got pulled over by a cop, and he was being a dick." Keep in mind, there's a difference between being a dick and being an *asshole*. The term asshole is usually applied to a person of equal or subordinate stature to yourself. An asshole is generally considered to be a person who is rude or abrasive for no particular reason. The key to the game is to always be fair in dealing with people, including your significant other.

And in relationships, there comes a time where you have to stand your ground and remain firm in your convictions. Even if that means you have to be considered a dick. Remember, it's best to have a female view you as a dick rather than look at you as being a pussy.

Switching Your Game Up

Women generally like the sense of security that comes with being in relationships, but they also like a little unpredictability. Familiarity breeds contempt. When you learn too much about a person, you become aware of traits and characteristics you may not like about that person. One of the most common characteristic people don't like in their significant others is *repetition.* We get tired of our mates doing and saying the same things all the time. For women, they will often complain about their men wearing the same clothes or the same underwear or wanting to go the same restaurants all the time,etc. For men, they usually complain about their women talking about the same subject, or repeating themselves over and over, which is the basic definition of nagging.

In most cases, people like to live vicariously through their significant others, especially women. And there are many women out there who feel like their lives are boring and mundane. If you are dealing with a female like this, you don't want to come across as a repetitive and predictable guy. Because the woman you deal with will often feel a sense of boredom because she sees too much of herself in that. So you have to sometimes switch your game up to give the relationship a jolt of adventure and unpredictability.

Now, switching your game up does not mean you have to be extreme. You don't have to act like Harry Potter one day and Ike Turner the next. The transition can be subtle. If your lady is used to you having a playful demeanor, start acting very serious for a few days and vice versa. If your lady is used to you having a playful demeanor, start dressing in suits and dress clothes for a week. The point is, when you switch your game up periodically, you create an air of mystery about yourself. Also, when you switch your demeanor back and forth, you make people cautious about disrespecting you or testing you. In many cases, women get bored and complacent in relationships and they try to test you in order to get some type of unpredictable reaction from you. But creating the Jekyll and Hyde persona will make it harder for people to manipulate or provoke you because they won't have a definitive angle on you.

Be Tactful about Changing Your Demeanor

You should always be as positive as you can be with your general demeanor. When you deal with others you should always be tactful in the way you administer the Mr. Hyde personality. This disposition transcends relationships and dating. For example, whenever I go to Las Vegas, I'm generally in a very positive state of mind. In many cases, when I go to the hotel casino where I'll be staying there is an undercover sales person greeting visitors as they walk in. Now many of these sales people are very nice, and they're very courteous. They will usually ask you if you're staying at the hotel, then they will ask you if you would like to get free tickets to see a show or concert while you're there in Vegas.

Now when I see these people my whole demeanor switches up. No matter how courteous they are, I put on the stone face, and I usually try to ignore them. Now on the outside looking in, it would appear that I am being extremely rude. The reality is, these sales people are really trying hustle you. They usually offer free tickets in exchange for you sitting through a two-hour high pressure sales pitch on buying a time-share,or something of that nature. I've found if you try to be a little courteous to these people, they will see it as a green light to try and hustle you and get a sale out of you even more. I've gotten to the point to when they step to me I turn into Mr. Hyde all the way. I don't give them any window of opportunity to think that they can pressure a sale out of me. This ideology has the same effectiveness when you're dealing with women in relationships. You initially present yourself as Dr. Jekyll to lure women in and to maintain your relationships, but you sometimes have to bring out Mr. Hyde to keep people in check.

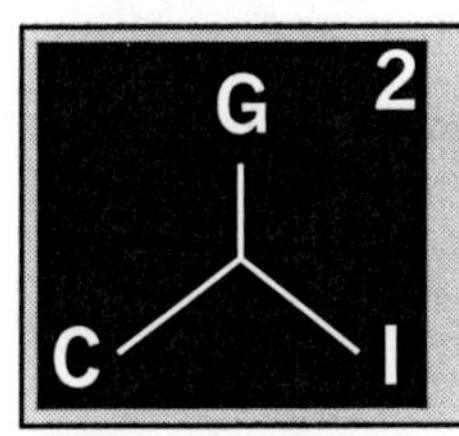

Rule Four applies to the element of GAME because it shows you how to use tactical personality changes to better deal with your mate

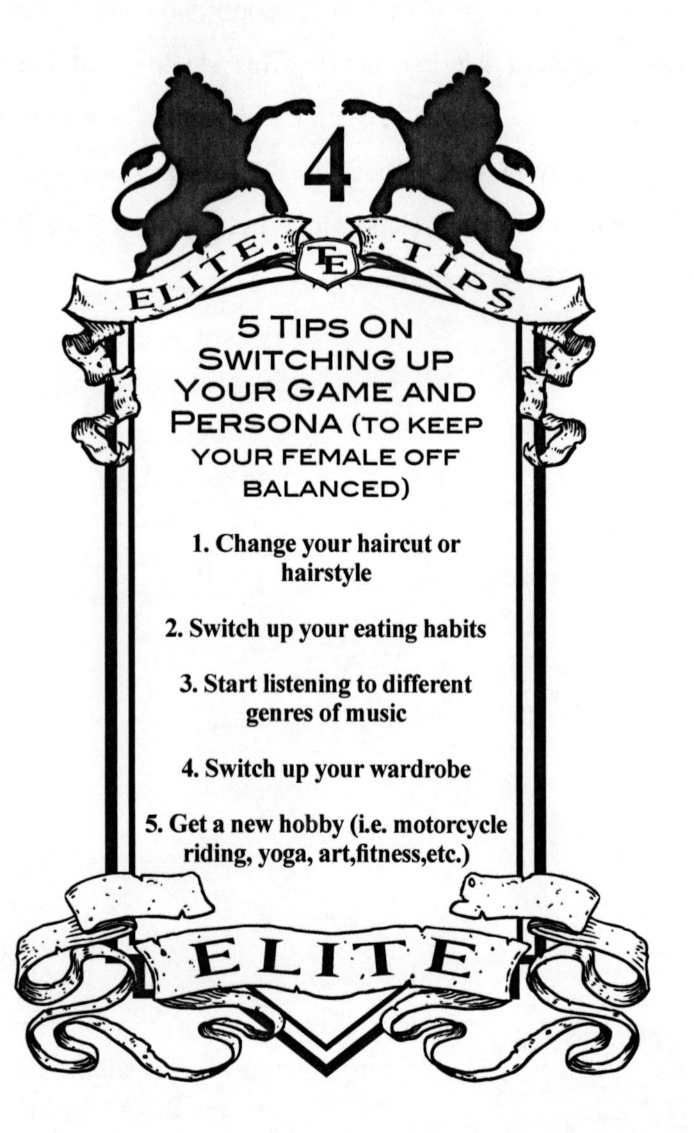
4
ELITE TIPS
TE
5 TIPS ON SWITCHING UP YOUR GAME AND PERSONA (TO KEEP YOUR FEMALE OFF BALANCED)
1. Change your haircut or hairstyle
2. Switch up your eating habits
3. Start listening to different genres of music
4. Switch up your wardrobe
5. Get a new hobby (i.e. motorcycle riding, yoga, art,fitness,etc.)
ELITE

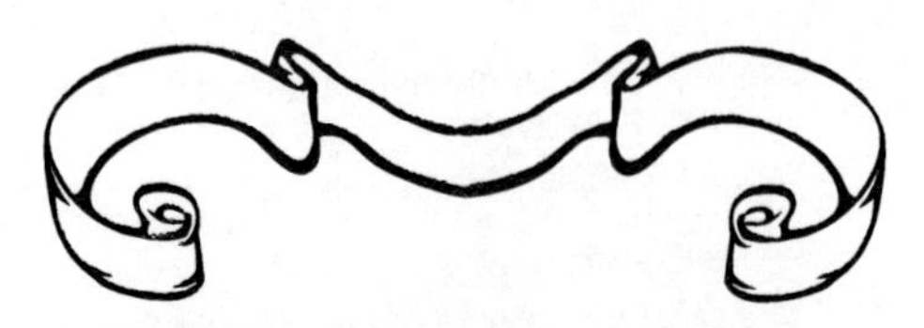

WHEN DEALING WITH PEOPLE,
REMEMBER YOU ARE NOT
DEALING WITH CREATURES OF LOGIC,
BUT CREATURES OF EMOTION.
— DALE CARNEGIE

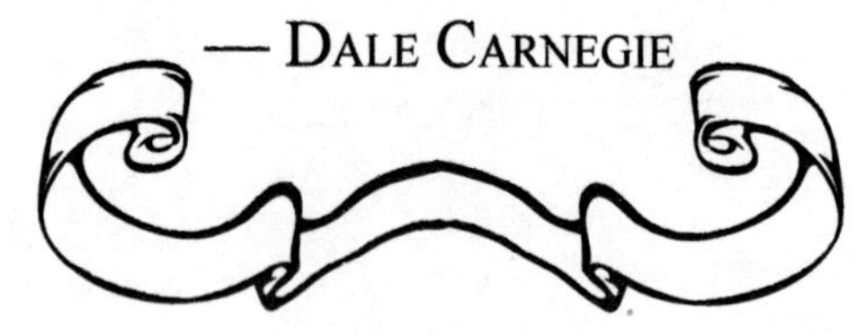

RULE 5

BLOCK THE TRANSFER OF FRUSTRATION

Sometimes when you are in a relationship, your woman may try to argue with you for illogical reasons or she might try to do things to try to push your buttons. For the most part, this is about her trying to transfer her frustrations onto you. There are two ways to generally deal with this situation: Defensively and Interactively. If you want to have peace of mind in your relationship, you're going to have to learn how to block that transfer of frustration. That's the defensive approach. You will also need to learn how to diffuse the build-up of frustration. That's the interactive approach. In order to effectively deal with this dynamic, you have to understand some of the root causes of frustration in relationships. **Here are the ten most common causes of frustration in relationships:**

ANNOYANCE	CRITICISM
INSECURITY	DISSATISFACTION
JEALOUSY	DISAPPOINTMENT
ANGER	A NEED TO CONTROL
EMBARRASSMENT	BOREDOM

Here's a breakdown of all ten of the root causes of frustration and how you can help diffuse them by getting into the good guy/Dr. Jekyll mindset.

ANNOYANCE

Sometimes in relationships, men can do a little too much cupcaking and smothering. When a female feels like a man is up under her a little too much, she will start showing symptoms of being slightly or blatantly annoyed. And the frustration from that will be transferred to you. In this case, you need to give your lady some breathing room by focusing on other activities such as hobbies, sports or anything else outside of the relationship.

INSECURITY

There are a lot of females who enter relationships with insecurities and a lack of confidence. And a lot times they'll base their level of confidence on their relationship with you. And whenever a female like this senses that there is any type of minor adversity in the relationship, they get frustrated and they begin to get extra clingy (which can be annoying to you). In this case, you can help diffuse the frustration by being a little more affectionate with her (but don't take it to the level where you are cupcaking with her) in order to reassure her that everything is cool in the relationship.

JEALOUSY

A lot of times when your female sees or suspects you of interacting with other females (i.e. running into your ex, getting text messages from women who are acquaintances, etc.) some feelings of jealousy may creep up on her. In many cases, your female doesn't want to let on to you that she has jealous feelings because she doesn't want to appear to be insecure. So all that pent up jealousy turns into frustration, and she will eventually project that frustration onto you. To help alleviate this, try to be as open as you can be about the nature of the interactions you have with other female acquaintances. You never want to be perceived as being deceptive. Let your female know that you have nothing to hide (that is if you actually have nothing to hide). Remember,the test of a true player is not how well he can sneak around with other women. It's about how honest and up front he can be about other women.

ANGER

Sometimes men get into relationships with women who are quick-tempered and seemingly mad at the world. A lot of men like being in relationships with these types of women because that anger can also be transferred into sexual passion. But on the flip side that anger can also turn into negative frustration. And the female will constantly try to transfer that energy onto you. To help curtail the frustration-from-anger dynamic with your female, just sit her down and have a serious conversation with her about the root of her anger. As I said before, relationships generally have problems for one reason – lack of effective communication. You would be surprised at how many problems you can solve in your relationship just by acknowledging that a problem exists. Find out if the anger is based on past failed relationships. Find out if the anger is based on something that happened to your lady as a child, and so on. Just getting your female to actually talk about why she's angry or what the underlying reason is for the anger will solve at least 50% of the problem.

EMBARRASSMENT

People usually become embarrassed for two reasons- something has made them self-conscious, or they have been exposed for something they tried to be deceptive about. Because frustration from embarrassment is so uncomfortable, people will quickly try to transfer that frustration onto others (usually by shifting blame, focus, responsibility, etc.). Now, if you are dealing with a female who has become embarrassed by a situation that was beyond her control, you can handle that situation in a gentle, Dr. Jekyll type of way. Just let her know that you are not trying to judge her and reassure her that you do have her back.

Now if you are dealing with a female that has done something deceptive and now she's embarrassed because she has been found out, that's when you tap into your inner Mr. Hyde. First, do not let her shift blame onto you. Also,let her know through your actions (and your words) that you are fully aware of the deception. Let her wallow in the uncomfortable vibe of embarrassment and frustration until you feel that she has learned the consequences of her actions. I will touch more on how to handle deceptive or disrespectful behavior in the next chapter.

CRITICISM

When a person feels like they have been judged or criticized, this usually makes them very defensive and frustrated. They will feel cornered and they will feel justified at lashing out at you, thereby transferring their frustrations. To help minimize this level of frustration with your female, simply give her an opportunity to explain her point of view of the situation without you giving off an interrogation vibe. Now if your female has done something that warrants criticism, then you have to get into Mr. Hyde mode and check her on it. Just because a female is frustrated by justifiable criticism doesn't mean her actions will be irreprehensible.

DISSATISFACTION

A lot of times women are simply dissatisfied with themselves. They might be dissatisfied about gaining weight, they might be dissatisfied about their hair, they might be dissatisfied about their occupation, etc. Sooner or later that dissatisfaction will turn into frustration and she will start looking for reasons to be dissatisfied with *you*. To help curtail this frustration before it can be projected, you should communicate with your female and help her figure out the specific reasons for her dissatisfaction. If it's a situation that can be rectified, you can help her figure out ways to do so. If it's a situation beyond her control, help her learn how to accept it and move on.

Disappointment

The root of dissatisfaction is disappointment. Sometimes when you are in a relationship with a female and she gets into a situation where something doesn't go her way, she will immediately try to transfer the frustration from that disappointment onto you.

Unlike dissatisfaction, which can be based on random instances that may or may not be beyond your control, disappointment is usually based on failed personal choices a person has made. In many cases, it is difficult for a person to take responsibilities for their failed actions because of:

a). the fear of failing again, and

b). all of the perceived energy they think it will take to rectify the failed action

So out of frustration, some people simply find it easier to shift the blame onto others. Don't let this happen to you in relationships. If you find that your lady is disappointed about something, let her know that the situation is a learning experience and try to get her to see the positive angle of the situation and move on.

A NEED TO CONTROL

In many relationships, the female feels that she has a need to control her mate. Some women do this because they abandonment issues. They feel if they can gain control over the man that they're with, this will lessen the chance of him leaving her. Also, a lot of women who were molested as children have a strong need to control their relationships with men.

When a person is violated as a child, this is a very traumatic experience that makes them feel completely powerless. So when a lot of these females become adults, they feel like they have to control every situation and the people around them. They do this so they will never have to experience that feeling of powerlessness again. The ironic thing is when a woman tries to control a man, the opposite effect will usually occur. Because this will usually push the man away and cause him to rebel in some form. And this will cause further frustration in the female.

When you're dealing with a female like this, help her pinpoint the timeline of the situation that contributed to her controlling behavior. Have her try to come to terms with it. Whatever you do, don't ever let your female try to control or dominate you in the relationship. Remember, if you let your female control or dominate you, she will eventually lose respect for you.

BOREDOM

In many relationships, women get frustrated simply because they have nothing else going on. Women have an innate desire for action, activity and adventure. If they can't find stimulation in a progressive way, they will get bored and try to find these activities by creating drama. Unnecessary drama is basically frustration from boredom. If you ever find yourself in a relationship with a bored drama queen, do not let her pull you into her realm of frustration. Help her find some activities to get into. Help her find a hobby or any other constructive activity to keep her mind occupied on something positive.

Defensively Blocking the Transfer of Frustration

Now that you have a general understanding of how to interactively prevent and diffuse the transfer of frustration before it is projected onto you, you now need to learn how to defensively block the transfer of frustration. To prepare to do this you have to first tap into your inner Mr. Hyde. Sometimes tension will build up in the relationship to the point where you can't even rationalize with your mate. A lot of women have emotionally based frustrations, and when you're dealing with this, the logical Dr. Jekyll approach just won't cut it.

Have you ever been in an argument or disagreement with a female and you know that you're making all the sense in the world, but the female's argument becomes more and more illogical? Women do this as a control mechanism. Women know the illogical premise of their argument will alter your mind state and cause you to become frustrated.

When negative energy builds up, it is extremely uncomfortable. That's why we have to immediately find ways to transfer it. If you were to stump your toe on a table leg or chair, for a split second while you're in pain, you might find yourself getting mad at the chair. And it's just an inanimate object. That's how strong the desire to transfer negative energy is. We will find anything, any object or any person to transfer that energy to. And when you are in a relationship, your significant other becomes the prime target for your frustrations.

So whenever you find your female trying to argue in circles, trying to nitpick with you, trying to nag you or trying to bicker with you for illogical reasons, do not feed into it. Laugh it off. Let her know that you are not taking her seriously at the moment. Don't even validate that type of behavior.

Allowing a female to get you angry or frustrated only validates this type of behavior. Always appear to be above petty, illogical arguments. When your female tries to illogically transfer her frustrations onto you, simply ignore the bait. Blatantly change the subject.

In many cases you don't have to be in an argument for her to try to transfer her frustration onto you. For example, if a guy is in a good mood and his female has a hint of frustration that needs to be transferred, she might make a slick or sly comment to him to get him out of his zone. A guy might be excited about getting a promotion at work. He might try to share this information with his female and she will purposely try to burst his bubble by saying something like, "What's so good about getting a promotion at such a dead end job like that anyway?" or something of that nature.

When women make seemingly innocent comments that are really designed to hit you below the belt, this is their way of transferring the frustrations from their own shortcomings onto you.

Now, sometimes women will take things past the transfer of frustration and try to say things that are outright disrespectful. When that happens, you have to handle the situation in a totally different way. More on that in the next chapter.

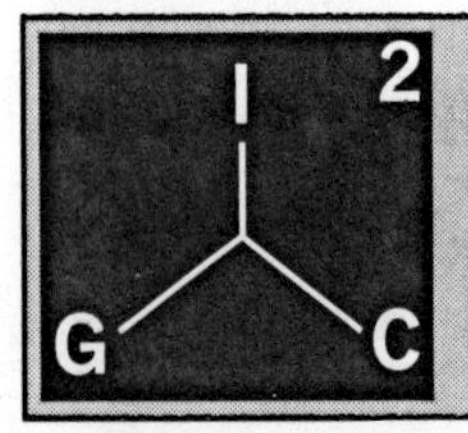

Rule Five applies to the element of INTELLIGENCE because it teaches you how to correctly analyze your female's behavior

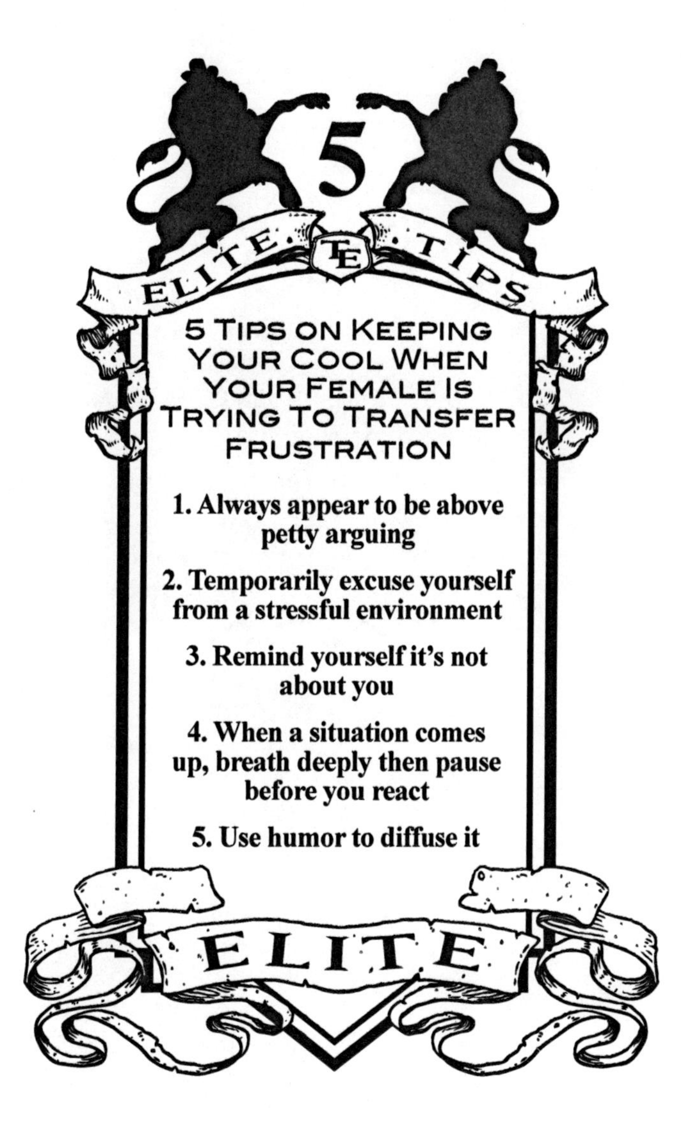

5 Tips on Keeping Your Cool When Your Female Is Trying To Transfer Frustration

1. Always appear to be above petty arguing
2. Temporarily excuse yourself from a stressful environment
3. Remind yourself it's not about you
4. When a situation comes up, breath deeply then pause before you react
5. Use humor to diffuse it

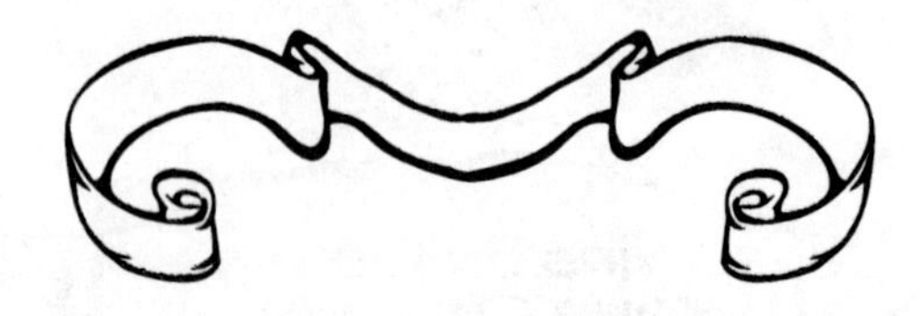

THERE IS BUT ONE CAUSE OF HUMAN FAILURE. AND THAT IS MAN'S LACK OF FAITH IN HIS TRUE SELF.
— WILLIAM JAMES

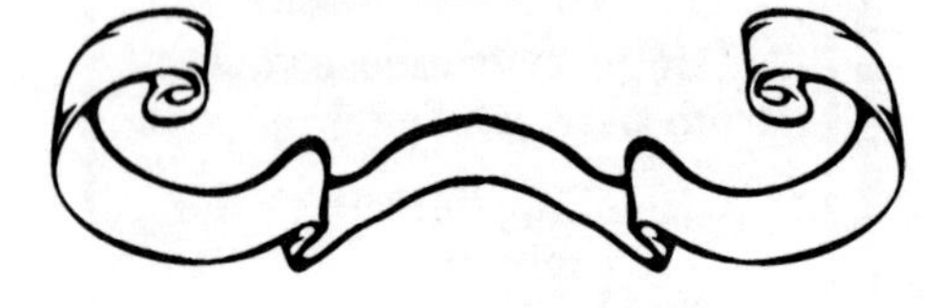

RULE 6

DO NOT TOLERATE DISRESPECT

Women like to test men. Plain and simple. This has been going on since the beginning of time. Whether we like it or not, some women will test men just to see how much they can get away with. As men, we cannot always control whether or not we will get tested by women.What we can control is how we react to the female who is trying to test us. In many cases, women can't help but to test men. It's almost in their nature.

Women are used to men giving them unwarranted praise, attention and accolades. This is based on the fact that many men want to have sexual relations with these women. Many women will go their entire lives, in and out of relationships without ever having their behavior regulated or checked. This causes many women to have a subconscious lack of respect for certain men. Many women don't like to admit it, but deep down they want a man to stand up to them and check any unregulated disrespectful behavior they might display.

The Subconscious Desire to be Disrespectful

Some women are victims of their own emotions, and they end up sabotaging all of their relationships with men by being disrespectful. This cycle can sometimes become so ingrained in a female's behavior she will often feel like she literally cannot control herself as far as being disrespectful to men. Sometimes women like this need to be saved from themselves. When the emotional desire to be disrespectful takes over their minds, they consciously want to be checked even though their subconscious mind is driving their behavior.

To be fair,we have to acknowledge that not every woman tests men and not every woman is disrespectful. But if you happen to get into a relationship with a female of this nature, you're going to have to learn to deal with this behavior effectively. In some cases, women show signs of disrespectful behavior right when you meet them. In other cases, some females put their best foot forward and then display disrespectful behavior as they feel secure enough in the relationship to do so. In any event, all forms of disrespect from women should be acknowledged and checked because letting disrespectful behavior escalate could lead to a potentially dangerous scenario. A woman will do what a man allows her to do. And many women think it's cool to be disrespectful because so many other men have allowed them to be disrespectful. You have to let women know through your actions that you're not one of those types of men.

There are three general categories of disrespect. And within those three categories, there are seven levels of disrespect. The three general categories of disrespect are:

Subtle (level 1-2)

Blatant (level 3-5)

Dangerous (level 6-7)

In many relationships, the disrespect from women will often start off small. If this behavior isn't checked, it will gradually escalate more and more to different levels. There are seven basic levels of disrespect that women give men in relationships. You never want the levels to increase to the point of no return. Because the higher up the levels go, the more you put yourself in jeopardy mentally, financially, emotionally and even physically. The worst and most dangerous situation to be in, is when you are around a person who has no respect for you. Respect is the foundation for every successful relationship. And it doesn't matter how elaborately built a relationship seems to be on the outside, if it is not built on the foundation of respect – just like a house that's built on a weak foundation – it will all come crashing down.

The following is a list of the seven levels of disrespect and how each level can escalate to the next:

Level 1 – Combativeness

A very subtle form of disrespect is when your female becomes very combative with you about general things. Females who display patterns of Level 1 Disrespect will make it a point to purposely disagree or find fault with everything you say or do. For example, if you say you want to go to a seafood restaurant, she might say she wants to go to a Mexican restaurant. If you say you want to go to see an adventure movie, she might say she wants to go see a comedy. Now, there's nothing wrong with couples disagreeing with one another about certain things, but if you find that your female is disagreeing with you about every little thing, this isn't an innocent coincidence. This is her passive-aggressive way of being rebellious and defiant to you. And when a female see that her defiant attitude and combativeness is going unchecked, in her mind, this gives her the green light to go to Level 2.

Level 2 – Slick Comments

Sometimes women will show disrespect to the men they are in relationships with by making slick, sly comments. A man might say to his lady something like, "I'm thinking about starting my own business." And his female, who is on the second level of disrespect, might say something like, "Yeah, right," or, "Whatever." Whenever your female starts to repeatedly make smart mouthed, sarcastic or slick comments during general conversations, you have to nip this in the bud before it escalates to Level 3.

Level 3 – Insults

When your female sees that she can get away with making slick comments to you, she will up the ante by blatantly insulting you. You might be having a conversation with your female then out of the blue she will say something like, "You're stupid," or, "You sound like an idiot," or something to that effect. Some women might pretend that they are insulting you in a playful manner at first, but do not be fooled by this. The insults usually start off playful at first so the female can test and see how far she can push the envelope. Once she feels like she will not be checked on her insults, her tone will become less and less playful. A common insult that many women like to administer is an attack on a guy's manhood. When a woman says things like, "You're a punk," or, "You're not a real man," or, "Stop acting like a bitch," etc., you have to check this behavior immediately because if you don't she will step it up to Level 4.

Level 4 – Public Embarrassment

When a female sees that she can get away with insulting you at home, she will then start disrespecting you by insulting you in public places. She might do things like loud talk you in restaurants, she might try to boss you around at the mall, or she might yell at you in front of strangers. Some women really put the public displays of disrespect on thick because they know that it is somewhat socially unacceptable and politically incorrect for a man to retaliate against or verbally check a woman in public. When a female feels like it's okay to embarrass you in public, she will take her disrespect to the next level.

Level 5 – Slander

Level 5 Disrespect is when a woman will not only disrespect you when you two are around other people, but she will start disrespecting you even when you are *not* around. This form of disrespect occurs when your female is slandering your reputation among friends, family and associates. She will get around her friends and family and say things behind your back like, "He is so dumb," or, "His sex is terrible," or, "He gets on my nerves." Some women will even go to *your* friends and family members and start trying to slander your reputation with them.

I have had friends in the past whose wives and girlfriends have called and emailed me telling me private and negative things about their relationships. These women do this under the guise of seeking outside help and advice for their relationships, but in reality, these types of women will put your business in the streets simply to embarrass you and to show their lack of respect for you. When a female feels like she can slander your name and reputation and not be checked on it, she will then step up to the next level of disrespect.

Level 6 – Infidelity

When a female sees that she can get away with other levels of disrespectful behavior on a regular basis, she will eventually commit one of the ultimate acts of disrespect in the relationship – she will go out and have sex with another guy (or guys). In many cases, when a female is engaging in the 6th level of disrespect, she will begin to get bold with her infidelity. She might do things like talk to other men who she's having sex with on the phone in front of you. Some women will even bring some of these so-called "guy friends" who they are creeping with, around you in person. A lot of females get a feeling of personal amusement to have a boyfriend or husband standing around clueless, while unbeknownst to him he's the butt of a perverse inside joke between her and her F-buddy.

In many cases like this the female will even start to leave clues to her infidelity. She will leave home for a few days without giving you an explanation. She will start talking about certain guy friends a little too much. She will leave phone numbers and business cards from different guys she has encountered lying around the house. When a female has become this blatantly disrespectful, they want either one of two things: A. They are desperately trying to get you riled up to the point that you will check them on their behavior or B. They are totally dissatisfied with the relationship, but they will feel guilty to break it off with you when you haven't really done anything wrong. So, they will engage in extremely disrespectful behavior so that you will get upset and break up with them. Either way, Level 6 Disrespect is very dangerous territory for you in a relationship. If a man won't take the hint and bail out of the relationship at this level, the female will up the ante to the next, last level.

Level 7 – Physical Harm

When a female starts to blatantly commit acts of infidelity and start flaunting it in your face, this shows that she has zero respect for you. And if this behavior goes unchecked, disrespect will eventually turn into contempt. When a person has contempt for you, this puts you in a potentially dangerous situation. Because at this point, the female you are with will start hoping and plotting for your failure, demise or downfall. Some women will get to the point where they will actually start to slap and punch you. Many women do this because they know if you retaliate they can call the cops on you and it will be their word against yours. In most cases of domestic violence the police will side with the female.

In other scenarios, when these women start interacting with other men on an intimate level, it is inevitable that they will begin to be influenced by these other men. And eventually, your female and these other men she is dealing with may start plotting with each other to find ways to cause you physical harm. Females like this will get you jumped, they will get you set up to be robbed and in extreme cases, they will even get your killed.

We have all seen stories on the news where seemingly mild-mannered soccer moms or church-going housewives will get busted trying to hire a hitman to kill their husbands so that they can collect the insurance money,or things of that nature. You never want to get to this level of disrespect in your relationships.

Why Men Allow the Levels of Disrespect to Escalate

There are a number of reasons why some men will allow their females to disrespect them on so many levels. Some men don't have enough self-esteem (the chapter I did on getting confidence from within should help men in this category rectify this problem). Some men are just clueless and don't even realize that they are being disrespected until it is too late.

Some men are fully aware that they are being disrespected, but they don't want to risk losing the female, so they will tolerate it. The reality is you should never let the disrespect from your woman escalate past Level 3 – Insults .If the levels escalates higher than that, it becomes extremely difficult for you to regain any level of respect again. If you really want to be thorough in your relationships, you don't let the disrespect get past Level 1. The earlier you check disrespectful behavior from your woman the better.

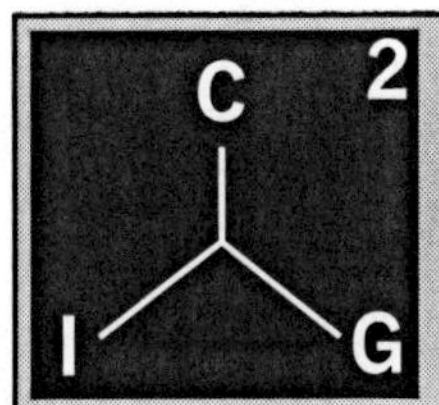

Rule Six applies to the element of COMMON SENSE because it shows you how to react to obvious behavior patterns of your mate

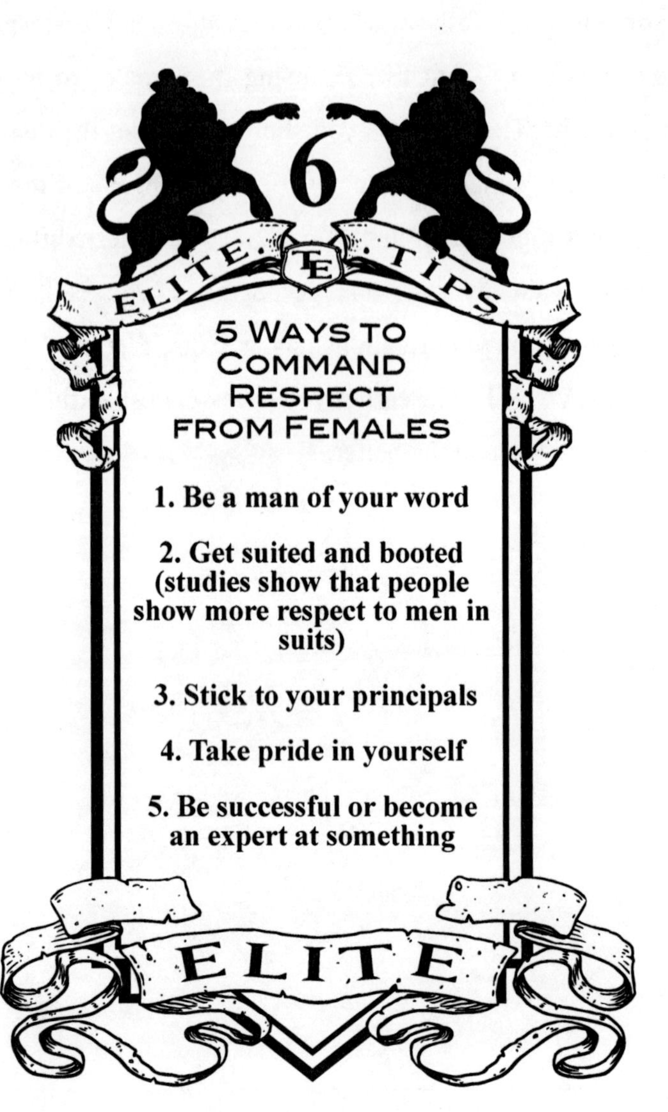

5 Ways to Command Respect from Females

1. Be a man of your word

2. Get suited and booted (studies show that people show more respect to men in suits)

3. Stick to your principals

4. Take pride in yourself

5. Be successful or become an expert at something

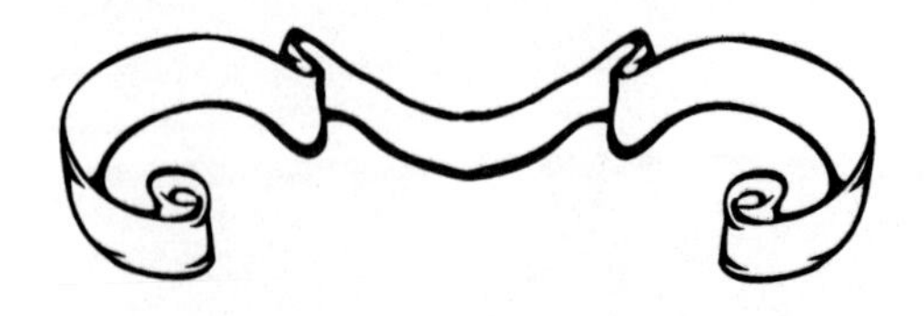

Unlike femininity, relaxed masculinity is at bottom empty, a limp nullity. While the female body is full of internal potentiality, the male is internally barren. Manhood at the most basic level can be validated and expressed only in action.
— George Gilder

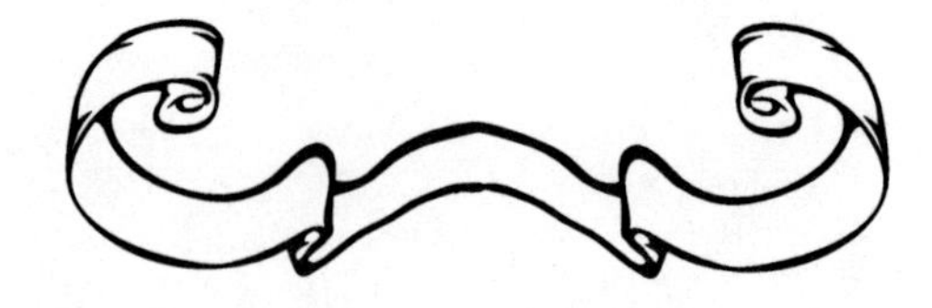

RULE 7

AVOID THE HEN-PECKED DYNAMIC

When a man becomes hen-pecked, he usually takes on the submissive, subservient role in the relationship. The basic definition of being hen-pecked is when a man is continually harassed or tormented by the persistent nagging of his woman. In essence, a man becomes mentally dominated by cohabitating within a hen-pecked dynamic. As I've implied earlier, a man should never allow himself to be dominated by his female. This will cause the female to eventually lose respect for him (and by now you know the ramifications of being in a relationship with a female who has lost respect of you).

Society tries to make it seem like the hen-peck dynamic is just the natural order of westernized relationships. For decades, cartoons, commercials, TV shows,and films have depicted American men as subservient schmucks whose lot in life is to be controlled by domineering women. A few examples that come to mind are comic strips such as Andy Capp, Dagwood Bumstead, TV shows such as *Roseanne*, *Everybody Loves Raymond* and movies like *Norbit* and countless others. The reality is, nothing could be more unnatural than a man taking on the submissive, hen-pecked role in the relationship. Men are supposed to be natural leaders in their relationships with women. So how do men end up being hen-pecked and dominated by their women? In order to answer that question we have to look at the mindset of certain types of hen-pecked men.

Some hen-pecked men are simply self-conscious and insecure about their looks, physical stature, financial situation, etc., so they will tolerate being in a relationship with a domineering female because they feel like they have no other options. They figure being with an angry, nagging, domineering female is better than being with no female at all. Now generally speaking, there are **five types of hen-pecked men**, they are:

<table>
<tr><td>The Daydreamer</td><td>The Pussy-Whipped Pansy</td></tr>
<tr><td>The Hulk</td><td>The Professional Trick</td></tr>
<tr><td colspan="2">The Masochist</td></tr>
</table>

Here's an assessment of these different types of men.

1. **The Daydreamer**

The Daydreamer is a guy who simply longs for peace of mind in his relationships. When the nagging and verbal abuse from his female starts, the Daydreamer has learned to mentally tune her out. Because he feels like his real life has become a living hell with the woman he's with, he often escapes to his own mental fantasy world where he daydreams about sports, traveling, other women and what life would be like without his ball-busting significant other.

In many cases, the Daydreamer was a mama's boy or a guy who grew up with a domineering female in his life. When he was a kid, he learned how to tune his mother out whenever she reprimanded or nagged him. And now as an adult, he has simply learned how to do the same thing with his wife or girlfriend.

If you want to maintain a proper balance in your relationship, ignoring or tuning your female out when she starts nagging will not always solve the problem. Sometimes that nagging has to be nipped in the bud. You have to check your female before that nagging behavior turns into blatant forms of disrespect.

2. **The Hulk**

The Hulk is an extreme manifestation of the Jekyll and Hyde Mentality. In the comic book world, the Hulk is a fictional character whose alter ego, Dr. Bruce Banner, gets accidentally exposed to dangerous gamma rays. As a result, whenever Dr. Banner gets angry or upset, he will transform into a giant, raging humanoid monster capable of random acts of violence. In the world of hen-pecked men, the Hulk is a man who forces himself to stay calm when his woman begins to nag him. He is aware of his temper and he knows that if he allows his woman to get under his skin, he might turn physically violent. And this will open up a whole new can of worms.

So, for the most part, the Hulk bites his tongue and struggles to keep his emotions in check throughout the relationship. He has to constantly talk himself down by repeating things under his breath like, "I'm not gonna hit her, I'm not gonna hit her," or, "I'm not gonna kill her, I'm not gonna kill her."

It's good to let things like petty nagging and bickering slide, and not to let your female push your buttons to a certain degree. But you do not want to constantly be under the pressure of holding back your emotions. If you let these emotions build up year after year, eventually you might snap mentally. You might end up doing something you don't want to do, so you have to communicate with your female that all the nagging is not an option. And for the sake and safety of your relationship, if you can't get on the same page with each other, you might have to charge her to the game.

3. **The Pussy-Whipped Pansy**

This type of hen-pecked male will tolerate the fussing and nagging from his woman simply because he does not want to put his sexual privileges in jeopardy. This is one of the most common types of hen-pecked men. In relationships, women generally have one main bargaining chip that gives them the upper hand – that's sex. The average man will allow himself to be manipulated by a woman who rations sexual favors as she sees fit. But an Elite Male, (such as yourself) is not average. He is **exceptional**. And the exceptional, Elite way to handle a female who is using sex as a bargaining chip is to trump her sex card. You do this by not sweating her for sexual favors. You have to discipline and teach yourself how to act indifferent to her sexually. Most women aren't used to this. When a man isn't sweating a female for sex it throws women off balance and makes them more intrigued. A man sitting around letting his woman talk to him any kind of way, afraid to put her in check because she might not have sex with him, is a show of weakness, and women are aware of this fact. If you want to remain on the Elite Level in your relationship, you must never come across as being mentally or sexually weak with your woman.

4. **The Professional Trick**

This type of hen-pecked male will tolerate the nagging behavior of his woman because in the back of his mind he has his own agenda. All the bitching and complaining from his lady gives him the justification he needs to spend his weekends cavorting with strippers, escorts and prostitutes, etc. This type of guy does not have affairs, so to speak. An affair is when a man is maintaining a secret, ongoing relationship with another woman. In many cases, these types of guys can barely maintain one woman let alone two. So, he saves up a certain amount of his money each week so he can trick it off on professional working girls.

And the nagging from his woman helps him relieve any guilt he may have about tricking with other women.

5. **The Masochist**

The term masochist or masochism is derived from a 19th century Austrian writer and journalist, Leopold von Sacher-Masoch. He was known (primary through his writings) for having an affinity for being dominated mentally and sexually by women. In modern relationships, some hen-pecked men allow themselves to be verbally abused simply because they secretly like getting dissed by women. In many cases, it becomes somewhat of a sexual and psychological fetish for these men to be humiliated and dominated by their women. Some of these men like the abusive behavior because they feel sexually and socially inadequate. Some of these men need someone to justify their self-loathing, and some of them are simply aroused by bossy women.

In the case of the masochistic, hen-pecked male, I would generally not advise him to change his situation because this is obviously a dynamic that gives him pleasure. If the situation works for you and you're getting satisfactory results, more power to you. But if you do decide to engage in this lifestyle, make sure your woman is in on the fetish.

You need to find a female with sadistic tendencies who gets as much pleasure inflicting pain psychologically, verbally, mentally and otherwise on men as you do receiving pain from women. If you get into a relationship with a non-sadistic female and try to constantly provoke her into nagging, humiliating and dominating you, eventually her tolerance for you will wear thin and she will lose respect for you. Then eventually she will sever her relationship with you.

Subtle Forms of Hen-Pecked Behavior

Some men might feel that they're not hen-pecked because their relationships do not display some of the more extreme examples I have just discussed. Just because your woman is not blatantly and obnoxiously nagging you or pestering you on an everyday basis doesn't mean that there aren't more subtle displays of hen-pecked behavior in the relationship. Here is a list of **five ways to tell if you might be hen-pecked in your relationship** and some tips on how you can correct this behavior.

1. If you are always apologizing

If you find yourself constantly repeating the phrases, "I'm sorry," or, "Yes, Dear," most likely you are hen-pecked.

Sometimes you have to let your Mr. Hyde surface and be an unapologetic male. Always acknowledging that you are wrong about something makes you come across as weak and unsure about yourself. Don't be afraid to put your foot down and stick to your guns.

2.**If your woman gives you a list of daily chores**

A man in a relationship who cooks and cleans every now and then is understandable. But if a female *requires* that her man cooks and cleans and does other chores on a daily basis, this isn't cool. As a man, don't allow yourself to be placed into a role reversal situation. You cannot be the king of your castle if you're constantly walking around with an apron and a mop in your hand. Don't be afraid to refuse to do unnecessary chores (meaning chores your woman can do herself). Now, if you and your lady are in a situation where both of your schedules make it more practical for you to take care of certain errands and things around the house, this is justifiable. But if your woman has you doing chores simply because she doesn't want to do them herself, you need to stop this dynamic immediately.

3. **If your woman only performs sexual favors on special occasions**

If your woman only performs oral sex for you on your birthday or if she only lets you hit it doggie style on Christmas, then you are definitely hen-pecked. Only a hen-pecked man would go along with this dynamic. Here's a secret: When women say they don't like to do certain freaky things sexually, most of the time this is B.S. Most women have an uninhibited, sexually adventurous side to them, but most men don't know how to bring that side out of them. If you are allowing a female to ration her sexual favors to you, this shows that she is running the relationship. You have to switch the game up and get her to be sexually open on a regular basis.

4. **If you have to hold your woman's purse at the mall**

Here's the deal – no matter what she says, your woman does not need to have you holding her purse for her AT ALL. If you're one of these guys we see sitting inside the mall looking bored holding a Coach bag, then you are definitely hen-pecked. Women trick men into holding purses because this is their low-key way of marking their territory. In some cases, women get men to hold their purses in order to emasculate them. Some women like to test men and see how well they can train them. Women are fully capable of functioning at the mall, at department stores, in dressing rooms, and at shoes stores with their purses in their possession, without your assistance. They do it all the time by themselves. So when a woman tries to innocently get you to hold her purse, simply refuse to do it. It may ruffle her feathers at first, but she will respect your manhood in the long run.

5. If you need permission to leave the house

If you are in a relationship and you inform your lady of your schedule and your whereabouts, this is perfectly normal, but there are some men who literally have to get *approval* from their woman before they can do anything. I know it sounds crazy, but I've seen this firsthand. I have had buddies in the past who were in relationships and they were supposed to hang out with the rest of the crew and then they would call up at the last minute saying things like, "Man, I can't go," or, "She said I can't hang out." If you have to get permission from your woman to do anything, you are hen-pecked, plain and simple, and you better upgrade your game in order to change this dynamic.

The Importance of Avoiding the Hen-Pecked Dynamic

The main reason you should avoid the Hen-Pecked Dynamic is because as a man you need to be able to think clearly and grow mentally. If you aren't growing internally, your relationship won't grow. A man cannot have peace of mind, think clearly or expand himself creatively or productively if his mind is constantly preoccupied with petty nagging and bickering from his woman. Also, a man cannot focus and be as productive as he can be outside of his home if he is constantly being emasculated by his woman within the home. This is why you should avoid getting placed into the hen-pecked bag at all costs if you want to truly have a well-balanced relationship.

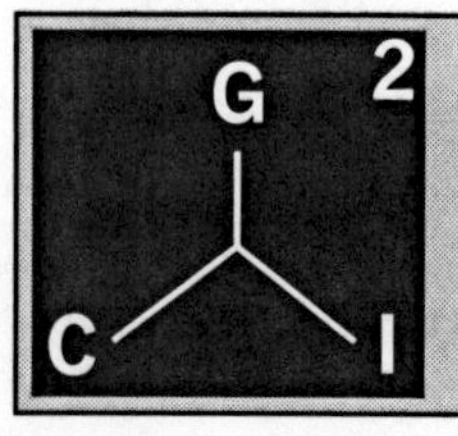

Rule Seven applies to the element of GAME because it encourages you to stay mentally focused in your relationships and not accept defeat

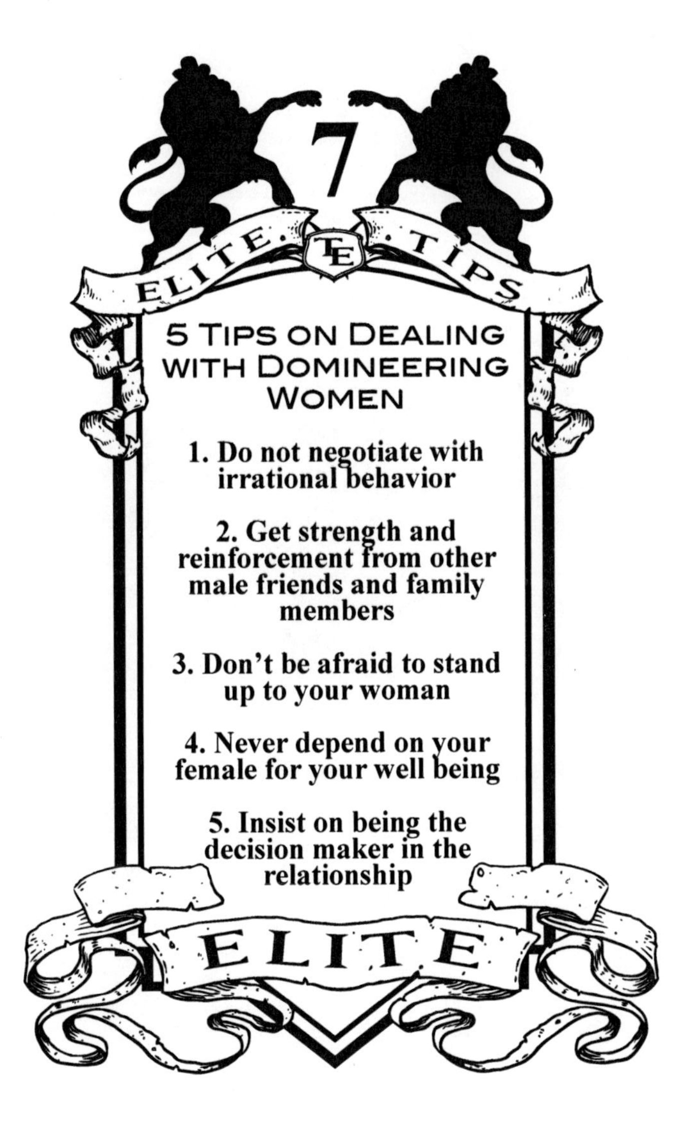

5 Tips on Dealing with Domineering Women

1. Do not negotiate with irrational behavior

2. Get strength and reinforcement from other male friends and family members

3. Don't be afraid to stand up to your woman

4. Never depend on your female for your well being

5. Insist on being the decision maker in the relationship

SECTION III

THE RECOVERY STAGE

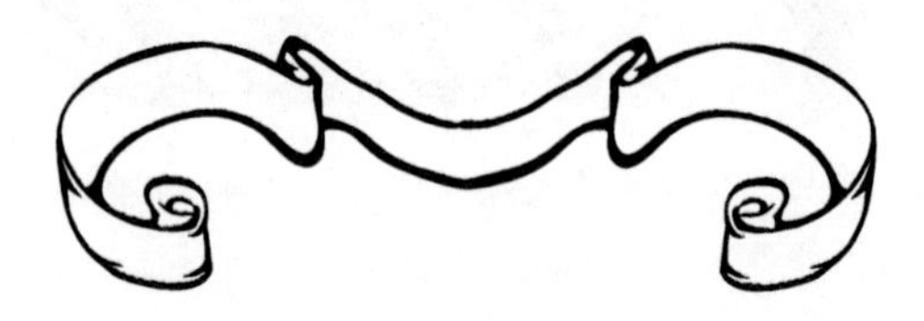

HE WHO TRIMS HIMSELF TO SUIT EVERYONE WILL SOON WHITTLE HIMSELF AWAY.

— RAYMOND HULL

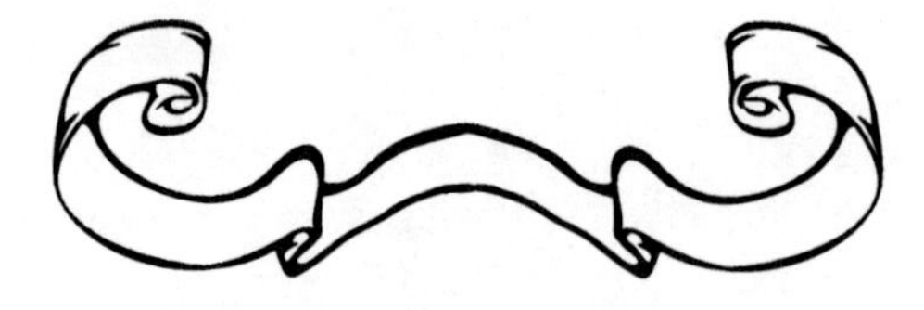

RULE 8

DON'T DEFINE YOURSELF BY YOUR RELATIONSHIPS

When we enter relationships we're usually optimistic and we hope for the best as we should. When we are in the initial stages of a relationship, the last thing we want to do is have a cynical outlook. The reality is in the back of our minds, we should always have a recovery strategy. We should be aware of the "what if" scenario – *what if the relationship doesn't work? What if she isn't the person I thought she was? What if I became single again?* Etc.

The best form of security is prevention. It's best to have a recovery plan before a relationship is severed than after it happens. When you try to think of a recovery strategy *after* the relationship is over, you end up making rash decisions that could negatively affect you for the rest of your life.

One of the best preventative measures you should implement before you reach a recovery stage is preventing yourself from being defined by your relationships.

Traditionally, men whose identities have been defined by their relationship have often been the subject of ridicule in our culture. We have heard countless jokes about men like Stedman, Kevin Federline, Chris Judd (J-Lo's ex-husband) Al Reynolds (Star Jones' ex husband) and other men in the public eye whose identities have been defined by the women they were with. One of the reasons for this negative stigma attributed to men who are defined by their relationships is because these men appear to have equal or subordinate status to their women. Men who are the leaders in their relationships usually command a certain air of respect. But men who are considered below their women financially or socially, or men who are not in a position to upgrade their women so to speak, are sometimes perceived as being soft.

Why People Define Themselves by Their Relationships

In many relationships, some men will give up their own individuality and begin to attach their identities to their significant other. There are three main reasons why men do this:

Low Self-Esteem

Pressure from Family and Peers

Branding and Marketing Purposes

Now, let's analyze all three reasons.

1. **Low Self-Esteem**

Some men feel like their own lives and characteristics are sub-par or uninteresting. And as I discussed earlier, these men feel they can only get confidence from being with women and getting in relationships. These types of guys feel that getting any woman to be in a relationship with them is an accomplishment. And that accomplishment becomes their identity. A guy like this loves to be known as "that couple" when he and his lady are referred to. This is the type of guy who will wear matching sweaters and outfits with his female on a regular basis. Younger men with this mentality will write "Jon Loves Kate" type drawings all over the place for the world to see. They will even get their woman's name tattooed on their body.

On a side note, men should never get a woman's name tattooed on them. It's okay to have a woman tattoo your name on *her* body. On the surface this may seem hypocritical, but there is a logical explanation for this. Getting a person's name tattooed on your body is a very submissive gesture, and a man should never take on a submissive position in the relationship. It's the woman's natural role to be the submissive participant in the relationship. If a man starts taking on submissive characteristics, the female will start losing respect for him. I know of several situations where men have gotten women's names tattooed on them and the women ended up leaving them shortly thereafter. Women like somewhat of a challenge in the men they deal with. Being a submissive male diminishes the challenge, which is why you never make submissive gestures like getting a woman's name tattooed on your body. And you don't want your self-esteem to drop to the point where you are defining yourself through your relationships.

2. Pressure from Family and Peers

One of the main reasons many men define themselves by their relationships is because of the pressure from family members and peer groups. Oftentimes, people close to us try to persuade us to follow a pattern that they feel is socially acceptable. Your family and friends will often pester you into believing you should be married by a certain age or you should start a family by a certain date. And because many people have a programmed desire to please their parents, siblings and other peer groups, they will start to conform to these requests. Some family members will even put on extreme forms of pressure and make it seem like there is something wrong with you if you haven't settled down yet within a certain time frame. They will also try to make you feel like you aren't really significant unless you are in a committed relationship or married. In order to stifle the complaints from their family and friends, some men will become Mr. Relationship. These types of men will go out of their way to display their relationship status in order to accommodate the desires of their loved ones. In doing so, their identities become defined by their relationships.

3. Branding and Marketing Purposes

This is the only situation where defining yourself by your relationships is justified. If you are a public figure or if you have a business endeavor that requires you to be associated with your mate for marketing purposes, this is understandable. For years there have been couples who built their brand around their relationship, such as Sonny and Cher, Ashford and Simpson, Peaches and Herb, Will and Jada, etc. So, if you're in a situation where you and your female are using the image of your relationship to market a brand or generate money, this is okay because it serves a practical purpose. But if you work at Wal-Mart and your lady works at Taco Bell, there would be no practical reason to define yourself by your relationships.

Are You a Team Player or a Team Mascot?

If you are a man who defines himself through relationships with certain women, you will end up being a team mascot instead of a team player. In the professional sports world, most teams have a mascot. The team mascot is usually a person in a suit or costume that represents the team's brand and image (such as the San Diego Chicken, the Philly Phanatic, the Orioles Bird, etc). The mascot's purpose is to boost the spirit and morale of the team and the team's fans. The mascot wears the team's colors. The mascot wears the team's jerseys. It will dance and run around, shouting and cheering for the team. The mascot's whole identity revolves around it fully representing that one particular team, but when the game is over, the mascot basically becomes insignificant.

At this point, the mascot really has no identity. But the actual team players remain relevant and significant because they came to the team with their own identities. Even though they respect their team and they represent their team, their identities are not defined by their teams. This is why players can get traded to other teams and still stay on top of their game. This same dynamic happens to men in relationships. Some men become mascots for their relationships. They profess to the world their love and commitment to certain relationships and they let their relationship define their identity. Eventually they become dependent upon their relationships, and if their relationships happen to end, these men will feel like they have lost their identities. A team player will come into a relationship with respect and commitment but never a sense of dependency. A team player knows that if one relationship fails, he can dust himself off and go play just as well for the next team.

The Culture of Cupcaking

Defining yourself through your relationships is really an extreme form of cupcaking. A lot of men cupcake with women by being overly affectionate. Usually they do this by being touchy-feely, and they end up defining their identities through their relationships because they have a need for reassurance from women. A lot of men who do this extreme cupcaking , are really looking for a nurturing, maternal figure in the women they date or get into relationships with. Too much extreme cupcaking is detrimental to your relationship because you will inadvertently start to push your woman away.

Women want to see strength and leadership in the men they date. Some women hem and haw about how they want to be independent and how men should be more sensitive, etc., but they say this as a test. Women like to test and see if they can change you and flip your character. They want to know if you are a man who can stand up to them and keep your principles intact. When a man relinquishes his leadership role and relegates himself to being his woman's equal, she will accept this, but she will look down on him to a certain degree. When a man is up under his woman all the time, this makes him look weak. If you are always trying to do things like cuddle or hold hands with your female, this makes you look needy and co-dependent. Eventually you woman will get fed up with your cupcaking behavior and get out of the relationship.

This whole cupcaking culture of men in Western society is a relatively new phenomenon. In Eastern culture, cupcaking behavior in men is almost non-existent, and in American culture, this behavior didn't begin to surface until the late 1960s. Back in the day, men were romantic, men were chivalrous, but they really didn't cupcake with women. Men were not up under their women all the time, holding hands and snuggling and sharing PDAs (public displays of affection). Back in the day, the general collective mindset of the average male was that of a leader or head of the household. In the late 1960s, the feminist movement and the free love hippie movement became an influential force in American culture, and ultimately it became an influential force in the behavior of men. Men were taught to be more sensitive and less masculine. Men were taught to relinquish their "oppressive, patriarchal" role in relationships with women and become their equals. Eventually many men relinquished their equal status and settled on a subjugated existence. This is how many men came to be dominated by the women they date.

The Dangers of Domination

When something is dominated, it becomes redefined by the thing that has dominated it. Historically, when smaller countries were dominated by more powerful countries, the smaller country would often be renamed or redefined by the values of the conquering country. When ancient Kemet was conquered by Greece, it was renamed Egypt. When the area known as Maharlika was conquered by Spain, it was renamed the Philippines, (named after King Phillip of Spain). This same methodology happens in business as well. When a business becomes weakened, it becomes susceptible to being dominated or taken over by another business. Some people like to use politically correct terms like *merger* to refer to such tactics, but in many cases, these tactics are really takeovers. This was the case with Washington Mutual Bank. When the U.S. economy took a dive in 2008, Washington Mutual took a major hit it could not recover from. This created an opportunity for Chase Bank to move in and take over Washington Mutual. Now, all of the Washington Mutual Bank branches have been redefined and renamed to Chase Bank.

This same dynamic happens in relationships. If a man allows himself to be placed in a weakened position in relationships because of a lack of confidence or low self-worth, he opens himself up to be dominated by his woman. And ultimately, he will be dominated and defined by the relationship. When it comes to long-term relationships, and marriage in particular, you have to approach it like a business.

Now, don't get me wrong. Love, respect and commitment are important factors in marriage, but it's still a business. This is why lawyers, notaries, state and legal and business documents are involved. Even if you're not married, you still have to have a business mindset if you're planning to have a serious relationship with someone. If you're trying to conduct business with someone, each party has to bring some assets to the table. If you're coming into the relationship with low self-esteem, that's a liability. If you're coming to the relationship with feelings of co-dependency, that's a liability. If you're coming to the relationship with feelings of neediness, that's a liability. And just like any other business,if you are coming into a relationship with a number of liabilities, you leave yourself open to being dominated or taken over by your woman and your relationship. So, in order to counter this dynamic you have to be aware of all the positive attributes and assets that you possess so that if your relationship happens to go south, your feelings of self-worth will remain intact and you will still have the confidence to do business elsewhere.

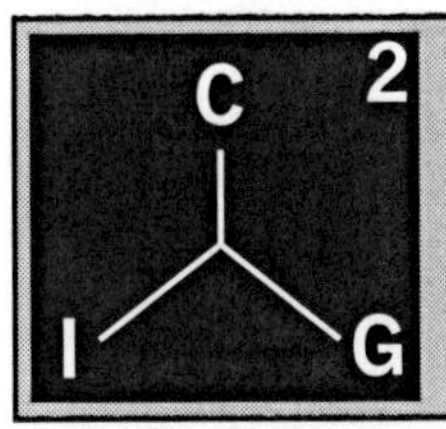

Rule Eight applies to the element of COMMON SENSE because it teaches you how to approach relationships in a practical way that works best for you

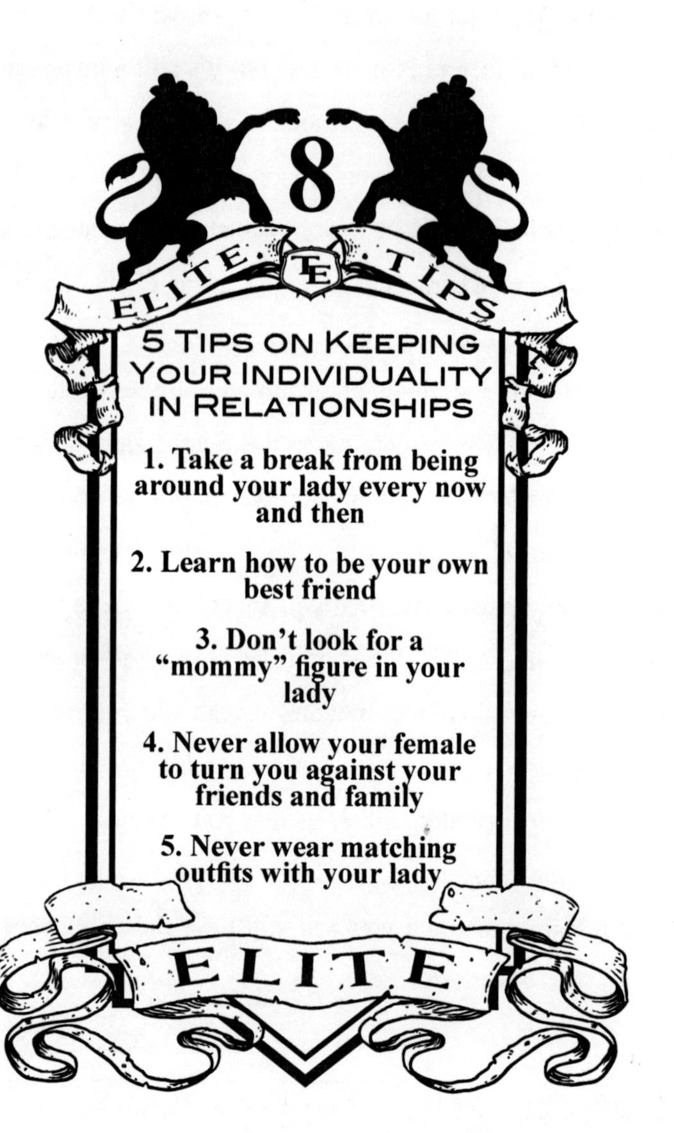
8
ELITE
TE
TIPS
5 TIPS ON KEEPING YOUR INDIVIDUALITY IN RELATIONSHIPS
1. Take a break from being around your lady every now and then
2. Learn how to be your own best friend
3. Don't look for a "mommy" figure in your lady
4. Never allow your female to turn you against your friends and family
5. Never wear matching outfits with your lady
ELITE

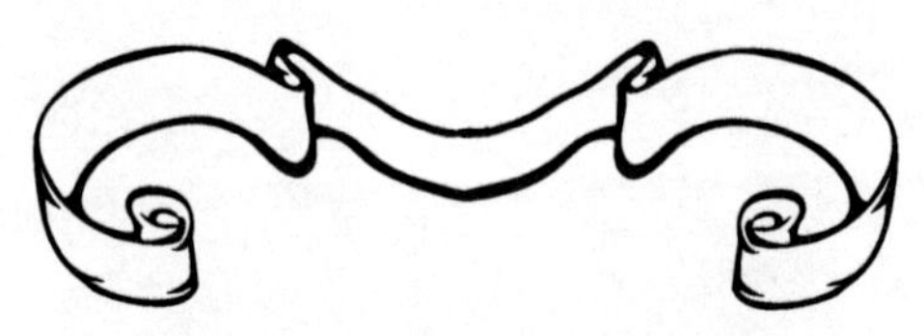

HANGING ONTO RESENTMENT
IS LETTING SOMEONE YOU DESPISE
LIVE RENT-FREE IN YOUR HEAD.
— ANN LANDERS

RULE 9

ACCEPT WHEN IT'S OVER

One of the most important aspects of recovering from a lost relationship is accepting when it's over. In many cases, people tend to drag out an inevitable break up. They do this until all their emotional resources are drained. As a man, when a situation just isn't working anymore, you have to learn how to charge it to the game. Remember, relationships and the dating game are like sports, and in sports, sometimes you win and sometimes you have to take a loss.

Why Is It So Hard for Some Men to Accept that It's Over?

Breaking up with a female will often make men feel angry, uncertain of themselves or frustrated. And just like women who are frustrated will try to transfer their frustration onto men, men will also try to transfer their frustration onto the women they are breaking up with. They will do this in the form of harassing phone calls, angry emails, uninvited visits and so on. Many men do this because it gives them a false sense of control. When these men feel like they no longer have control over the relationship, they will try to gain control over the female's emotional state by harassing and irritating her to a certain degree. Generally there are **four main reasons why some men have a hard time accepting when a relationship is over**. They are:

Insecurity

Sense of Losing an Investment

Embarrassment

Possessiveness

The following is an analysis of all four reasons.

1. Insecurity

Relationships by design, are based on having a sense of security – knowing that you consistently have someone who is there for you emotionally, physically and mentally. So when you break up with a person, you immediately lose that feeling of security. When a baby is held by its mother, it feels calm, safe and secure. When the mother sets the baby down, the baby will start crying and in some cases, it may start kicking and screaming. They do this because temporarily, they lose their sense of security. Grown men do the same type of kicking and screaming routine when they break up with a female. They might yell, they might cry, and they might even beg, because a sense of insecurity has taken over. And being insecure is an extremely uncomfortable feeling and emotion. Even when their relationships has clearly ended, these men will do everything in their power to regain that sense of security again.

2. Sense of Losing an Investment

When you are in a relationship, you invest a lot of time, energy, emotion and in many cases, money. No one wants to invest in something without having some type of return on their investment. If you invest in a business, you want a return on the profits. If you invest in real estate, you want a return of the equity of the properties. If you invest in a relationship, you want a return of whatever you feel like you have contributed. You may want a return of the loyalty you invested. You may want a return of the dedication or the commitment you invested. And in some cases you may want a return of the sex. So, if you have made an investment in a person, and they decide to walk away without giving you what you feel is a return on your investment, this could cause you to feel angry or betrayed. Even though the relationship is over, you will still try to correspond with your ex in a last ditch effort to salvage some type of emotional asset from them. Just like investing in stocks or real estate, you have to know when to cut your losses and move on.

3. Embarrassment

Many times when people break up in relationships, there's a strong feeling of embarrassment and shame that they feel. If they are coming out of a relationship that didn't work, they might feel that they have let their family and friends down in some way. Also no one wants to appear as if they have been dissed by their significant other in the eyes of their friends and family. So in order to save face and not be perceived as a failure by their peers, some men will still try to hold on to a barren relationship.

4. Possessiveness

Men are possessive creatures by nature. Some men know how to control their possessive nature better than others. But there are some men who refuse to accept when a relationship is over simply because they don't want another man to have their ex. In many cases, no matter how long a man has been broken up with his ex, he doesn't want to imagine her being with another man. And this is extremely true if a man has just broken up with a female. If a female appears to be rebounding from a recent break up, some guys will try to come back in her life just to throw salt in the next man's game.

Now when a man continues to display any of these four types of character traits- Insecurity, Loss, Embarrassment or Possessiveness- after a break up, he runs the risk of getting into another realm of dysfunctional relationship recovery.

Stalking

As I stated earlier, some men feel that if they can't get any love or commitment from a woman anymore, they will try to draw some other emotion from her, even if the emotion is negative.

In the minds of these men, any type of emotion or attention is better than none at all. Also men like this will try to sustain any type of connection with the female after the relationship is over. This usually results in stalking in the forms of threats, harassment and surveillance.

The ability to stalk people has become more sophisticated and easily accessible over the years. Back in the day, if a man wanted to stalk a female he had to pack up some snacks and beverages, get in his car, go over to the woman's house and wait in the bushes or sit in a tree for hours until the female came home. These days, stalkers have social networking sites, GPS devices, access to cell phone records and other types of techniques by which to keep track of unsuspecting females.

If you ever want to reach Elite status with your game, you cannot have any characteristics of a stalker. Some men may be stalkers and not even know it because when you think about it, no one ever admits to himself (or others) that he is a stalker. Many stalkers feel justified in their behavior. So, here's a list of **five ways to tell if you might be a stalker** or exhibiting stalking behavior after your relationship has ended with a female:

1. If you show up to her home or job unannounced

2. If you keep sending her unsolicited gifts

3. If you cause damage to her property (i.e., keying up her car, spray painting her house, slashing her tires, etc.)

4. If you call her family and friends trying to get information about her

5. If you create a fake Myspace or Facebook page to monitor her activity

Now, if you are in a relationship with a female and you feel like she might be engaged in some shady activities, it is definitely within your rights to want to investigate the situation. In this case, it is justifiable to check your lady's cell phone records or monitor her whereabouts because you don't want to find out that your female has been plotting behind your back when it's too late. But doing all of this after you have broken up with a female is stalking plain and simple. And if the relationship is over, you need to climb down out of the tree, get out from behind the bushes, throw away her Facebook password and move on.

Potential Reconciliation versus Stalking

Some men who are stalkers try to justify their behavior by telling themselves that they are simply trying to reconcile their relationship with their ex. It's okay to try to reconcile the relationship if there has been some type of miscommunication and both parties are willing to work things out. But when the reconciliation process is one-sided, this is stalking. And if a female is adamant about the relationship being over, charge it to the game. Don't chase 'em, replace 'em.

Stalking is useless energy. It's a waste of time. It only frustrates you and it chips away at your self-esteem. Plus, there are legal ramifications to stalking. If you are a man who's in the process of getting a divorce, you really don't want to venture into the realm of stalking because this could give your ex the incentive to file a restraining order against you. This could be used as leverage against you in court.

Bringing Closure to a Relationship

Whenever you keep contacting your ex telling them you need closure, this basically means that you are not over them, and it shows that you want to find a way to remain in the relationship. If you really want to get over a relationship, you have to get closure within yourself. Always try to come out of situation with dignity, because at the end of the day that's all you really have: Integrity and Dignity. These are the two things that cannot be taken away from you. You have to relinquish them. When a relationship is over, we often feel like we are losing control. Some people will compromise their dignity in an effort to regain control of the relationship, but sometimes there is dignity is letting go; charging things to the game. Never harp on a failed entity. A lot of a man's strength is in his ability to not let his emotion get this best of him.

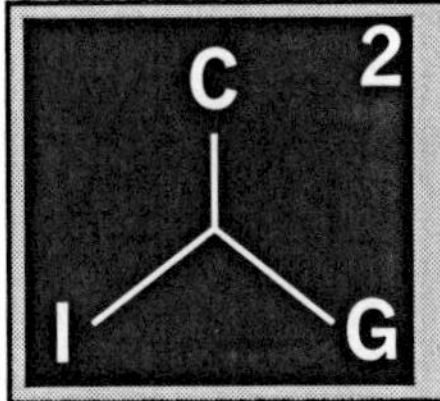

Rule Nine applies to the element of COMMON SENSE because it helps you use proper judgment when it comes to recovering from a break up

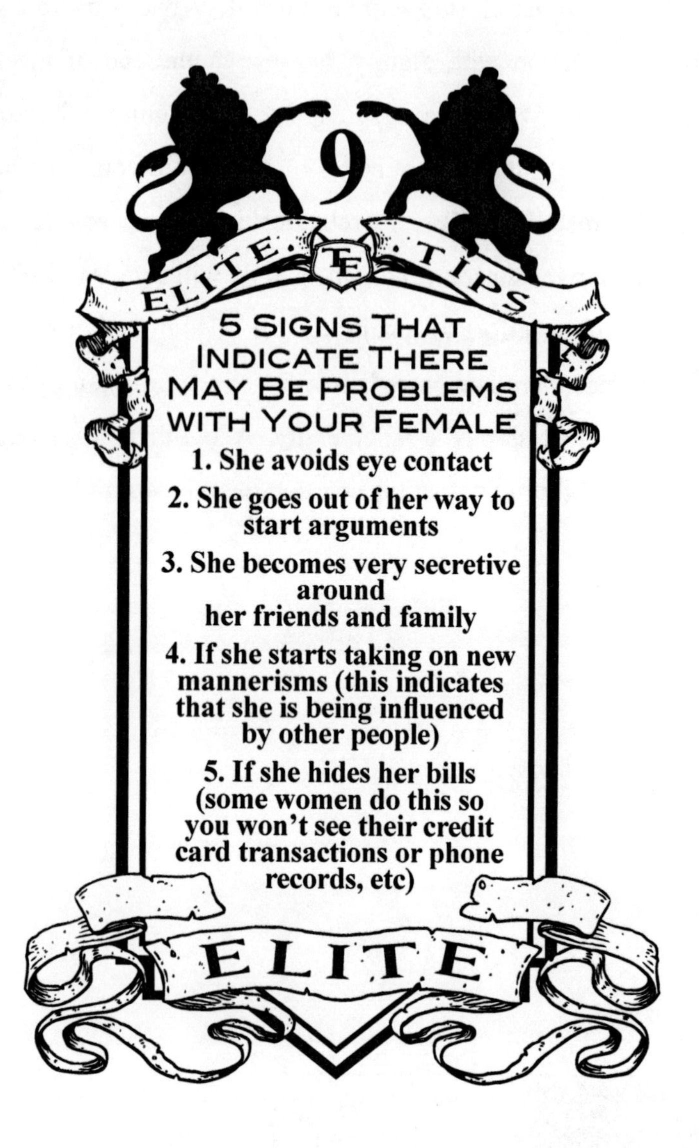
9
ELITE TIPS
TE
5 SIGNS THAT INDICATE THERE MAY BE PROBLEMS WITH YOUR FEMALE
1. She avoids eye contact
2. She goes out of her way to start arguments
3. She becomes very secretive around
her friends and family
4. If she starts taking on new mannerisms (this indicates that she is being influenced by other people)
5. If she hides her bills (some women do this so you won't see their credit card transactions or phone records, etc)
ELITE

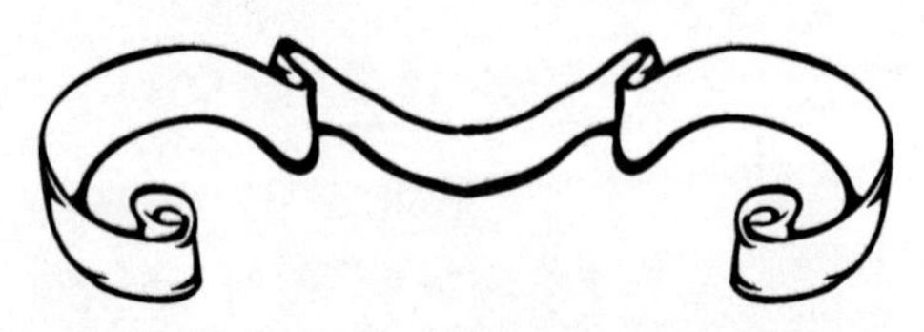

EXPERIENCE IS NOT WHAT HAPPENS TO A MAN. IT IS WHAT A MAN DOES WITH WHAT HAPPENS TO HIM.

— ALDOUS LEONARD

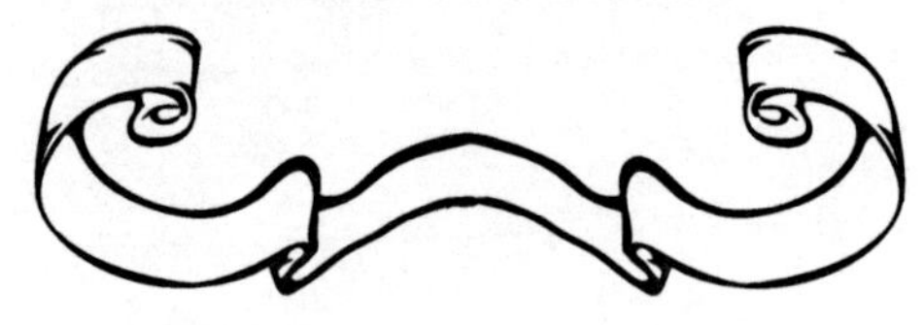

RULE 10

LEARN FROM EVERY RELATIONSHIP

One of the biggest setbacks for many men in the dating game is that they never learn from past mistakes. In life, whatever you don't complete you will repeat. If you don't complete the curriculum of a particular grade in school, you will have to repeat that grade. If you want to be an athlete and you don't complete the physical or athletic requirements of a particular sports team, then you will have to try out for that team again the following season. To complete anything in life you have to learn and adjust to a particular protocol; this includes relationships. If you never learn from past mistakes in relationships, you will repeat the same mistakes over and over again. And when you continue this process over a period of time, this will turn into mental and emotional baggage.

Carrying Negative Baggage

When men accumulate a "hate the world" mentality or a "women are no good" disposition, this causes them to consciously or unconsciously sabotage any potentially new relationship. This also causes them to sabotage their thinking. You will attract the things that you focus on, be it positive or negative. So if you tell yourself that all women are scandalous and no women can be trusted, then you're going find yourself gravitating toward these very women. This happens because in your mind, these are the only types of women that you think exist. Now, it's good to be cautious about dealing with new people. It's even good to be somewhat cynical, but don't be spiteful and bitter when you're going through the recovery stage. No quality female wants to be around a man with a negative vibe.

Don't Go Into the "Why Me?" Phase

A lot of times when guys break up with females, they start going into the "Why Me?" phase. They start thinking *why can other people have healthy relationships and not me? Why are other guys successful with women and not me? Why do women like other guys and not me? Why me, why not me?* And so on. There's a reason the word *why* sounds so much like the word *whine*. Asking the question why in an inquisitive context is constructive, but if you are continuing to ask the question "why" in a complaining manner, you then begin to come across as a whiner. And the basic definition of a whiner is *a person who complains in a feeble way*. If you are going through the recovery stage, you have to realize that you are not the only person who has been in a relationship that didn't work. Anyone who has dated two or more people in their lives has been in a relationship that didn't work. So, whining or getting into the "Why me?" phase over an extended period of time about something as common as a break up is retrogressive.

Don't Get Consumed by Anger

As I mentioned before, a lot of guys become bitter and angry after a break up and some men allow this anger to negatively affect how they interact with other women. If you are to reach Elite status in the game, don't ever become consumed by anger and don't let anger control you after a break up. Because over time, your ex female has more than likely moved on to the next relationship, and you're still letting your anger with her hold you back.

Upgrade Your Software

You should always use the recovery stage as an opportunity to upgrade yourself. Upgrading your game is like upgrading your computer software. In many cases, in order to upgrade something you need to have a clean slate to rebuild from. When you have software on your computer and you want to install an updated version of it, oftentimes your computer will prompt you to uninstall the old program. The computer acknowledges that if you run too many consecutive programs, it will cause the computer to not operate properly. This is the same with upgrading your game. You can't have a fresh start in a new, upgraded relationship if you're still carrying anger, emotions, frustrations, bitterness and grudges from past relationships. In order for you to function properly in a new relationship you have to uninstall your old software.

Jumping into New Situations

When you break up with a female it's cool to casually date and socialize, but you may not want to jump into a serious situation right away. As I mentioned before, often after a break up, a lot of our emotions tend to surface. This is normal. You should acknowledge these emotions so that you can get them out of your system. But you don't want to use these emotions, (such as revenge and spite) in order to jump into another serious relationship too soon. When you try to seriously date too soon after a break up, often you're not thinking too clearly and you open yourself up to making bad judgments. You might jump into a relationship too soon then after a while, when logic kicks in, you realize you're dating a weed head or a meth addict. Or you may end up getting someone you barely know pregnant or even worse- you might end up catching some type of disease. So, it's best not to blindly jump from relationship to relationship. As the old saying goes, look before you leap. And in this case, the thing you should be looking at is yourself and what's best for you in the long run.

Man-Up to Pain

Whenever we feel any type of physical pain, we usually do whatever it takes to alleviate that pain. If we have a headache, we will immediately take aspirin. If we have a scrape or a cut, we will apply a pain killing ointment to it. If we have a body ache, we will take prescription medicine. And people will often do the same for emotional pain. In order to not deal with emotional pain, some people will engage in drug use, promiscuous sex or compromising decision making in general. As I stated before, people will compromise their dignity and integrity in order to feel temporary relief from emotional pain. Some people will remain in denial about certain circumstances in relationships in order to avoid the pain of dealing with the truth. If you want to reach the Elite status with your game, you have to man-up to emotional pain.

In many cases, pain is growth. This is why we use terms like "growing pain." When children are teething, their gums become painful because their teeth are growing in, which is good for them. When you go to the gym and you work out, your muscles go through a painful recovery stage; this causes them to grow and make you more physically fit.

A lot of times we can't control what happens to us in some situations. When you take control of how you view certain circumstances that happen in your life, you will learn how to use pain as a tool for growth. So, if you feel like someone has hurt you emotionally in a relationship, own the emotion, then charge it to the game. Because the next step is to use that pain to grow and become a stronger, wiser, more experienced man.

Don't Play the Victim

Nothing is more unattractive to a potential female love interest than man playing the victim. No matter how wronged you feel about your last relationship, don't ever try to garner sympathy from other women when you are in the recovery stage. Remember, women want an Elite Male, a man who is on top of his game. Wallowing in self-pity and blaming others for things that happened to you is generally viewed as a feminine characteristic. As a man, you have to own up to the things that happen to you in life. Even if something wasn't your fault, per se, you still have to acknowledge your own role in the outcome of the circumstances.

When you break up with a female you have to ask yourself logical questions instead of emotional ones. When you are emotional, you will start asking yourself "Why me?" types of questions. But when you are being logical, you ask yourself more constructive questions, such as, *"Was I too dominant in the relationship?" "Was I too passive in the relationship?" "Was I too accommodating?"* Etc. Even if the break up was not your fault and you thought that everything was cool when she left, you still ask yourself things like, *"Was I observant enough? Did I ignore the signs?"*

On a side note, if you are in a relationship and you see that a break up is imminent, it's best for you to initiate the termination of the relationship yourself than to let the female break up with you. Whenever a man breaks up with a female, there's always a strong possibility that the female will regroup and try to come back to him in the future. Now whether or not you should accept the female back depends on the severity of the issue that caused the break up in the first place. But if the female initiates the break up, most likely she will not come back to you in the future.

Learn from It, Don't be Burned from It

Just remember that every relationship endeavor that you think is negative, is really a learning experience. If something doesn't go your way, don't be burned from it, learn from it. Allowing yourself to be burned from relationships is pointless and it's draining. But when you allow yourself to learn from these experiences, you grow and your game gets tighter. You will learn how to make better selections when it comes to women. You will learn what to tolerate and what not to tolerate in relationships. You will learn how to avoid certain pitfalls. You will learn how to read certain behavior patterns from your mate, etc. And gathering all this knowledge will make your game much more crisp for when you deal with the next female.

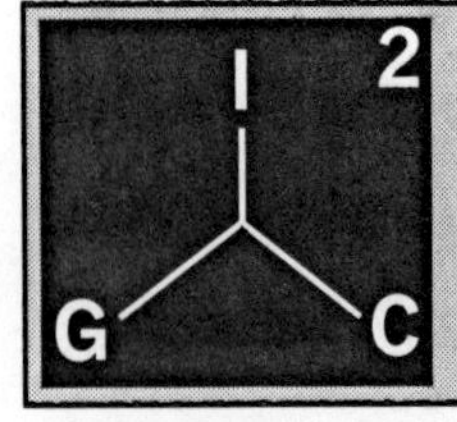

Rule Ten applies to the element of INTELLIGENCE because it explains how to gain knowledge from every relationship situation you engage in

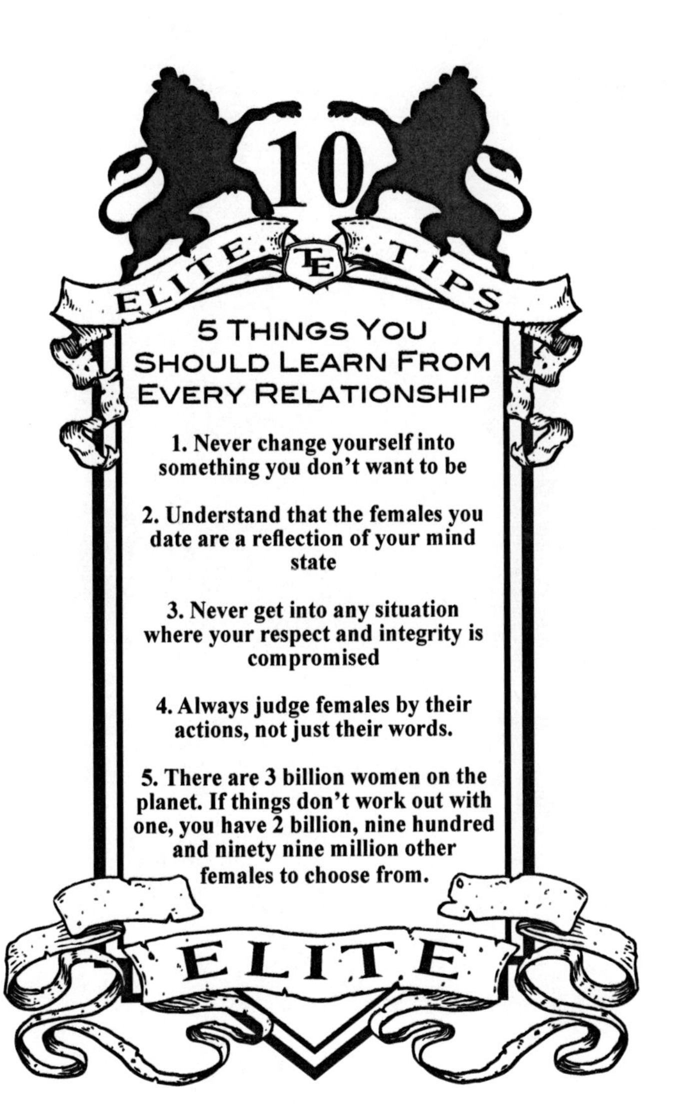
10
ELITE TIPS
TE
5 THINGS YOU SHOULD LEARN FROM EVERY RELATIONSHIP
1. Never change yourself into something you don't want to be
2. Understand that the females you date are a reflection of your mind state
3. Never get into any situation where your respect and integrity is compromised
4. Always judge females by their actions, not just their words.
5. There are 3 billion women on the planet. If things don't work out with one, you have 2 billion, nine hundred and ninety nine million other females to choose from.
ELITE

CONCLUSION

Now that you have a full understanding of all the rules you need to know in order to deal with women, here are ten more tips that will help you stay well-balanced with your game.

1. **BE TRUE TO THE GAME/**

   DON'T TRY TO TRICK OR DECEIVE WOMEN.

2. **ACCEPT SUGGESTIONS FROM WOMEN/**

   BUT NEVER TAKE ORDERS FROM WOMEN.

3. **TAKE THE INITIATIVE/**

   BUT DON'T ACT THIRSTY WITH WOMEN.

4. **BE YOUR OWN MAN/**

   BUT DON'T SEEK VALIDATION FROM WOMEN.

5. **LOOK WOMEN IN THE EYE WHEN YOU TALK TO THEM / BUT DON'T STARE WOMEN DOWN TO WHERE IT'S CREEPY.**

6. **BE ENTERTAINING/ BUT NEVER TRY TO IMPRESS WOMEN.**

7. **CONTROL YOURSELF SEXUALLY/ NEVER LET WOMEN USE SEX AS A BARGAINING CHIP.**

8. **VALUE YOURSELF AS A MAN/ DON'T PLACE WOMEN ON PEDESTALS.**

9. **MAKE INTEGRITY THE FOUNDATION OF YOUR GAME/ DON'T USE MONEY AS THE FOUNDATION.**

10. **RESPECT WOMEN WHEN IT'S EARNED/ BUT NEVER TRUST A HO.**

If you want to reach the Elite status in your game and remain at that level remember, you have to think like a leader. I cannot stress this point enough. Being a leader doesn't mean controlling people. If you notice, the sub-title of this book is called "Ten Rules Men Must Know in order to *Deal* with

Women," not *control* women. When a man tries to outright control women, this will often cause some women to rebel against him and act out in a passive-aggressive way. The way you deal with women effectively is by controlling your own behavior and not allowing yourself to be manipulated by women or circumstances that stem from relationships. If you want to be a leader you have to lead by example. You have to carry yourself in a manner that commands respect. Being a leader, you have to show that you have confidence to take the initiative when dealing with women. This doesn't mean chasing after every woman you see .Because in order to have a properly balanced relationship, you have to allow women to *choose* you. In order for this to happen you have to plant the seeds for the choosing process. You have to pro-actively entice the female to choose you. And the best way to do this is by carrying yourself a certain way. If you soaked up all the game in this book, you will know that there is only one way to carry yourself. That's the ELITE WAY.

ABOUT THE AUTHOR

TARIQ "ELITE" NASHEED *is an author/lecturer, television personality, and fashion designer who has appeared on TV shows such as The Tonight Show with Jay Leno, Late Night with Conan, and several shows for MTV and VH1. He is also the host of the critically acclaimed Mack Lessons Radio Show (macklessonsradio.com). Tariq does lectures all around the country teaching men and women his strategies and techniques on dating and relationships. Tariq lives in Los Angeles, Ca.*

CONTACT TARIQ ELITE AT:

INFO@TARIQELITE.COM

WWW.MACKLESSONS.COM

WWW.MACKLESSONSRADIO.COM

WWW.TARIQELITE.COM

WWW.FACEBOOK.COM/TARIQELITE

WWW.TWITTER.COM/TARIQNASHEED

WWW.MYSPACE.COM/TARIQELITE

Other Books By
Tariq "Elite" Nasheed:

*The Mack Within
(Penguin)

* Play Or Be Played
(Simon and Schuster)

* The Art Of Mackin
(King Flex Ent.)

*The Art Of Gold Digging
(King Flex Ent.)

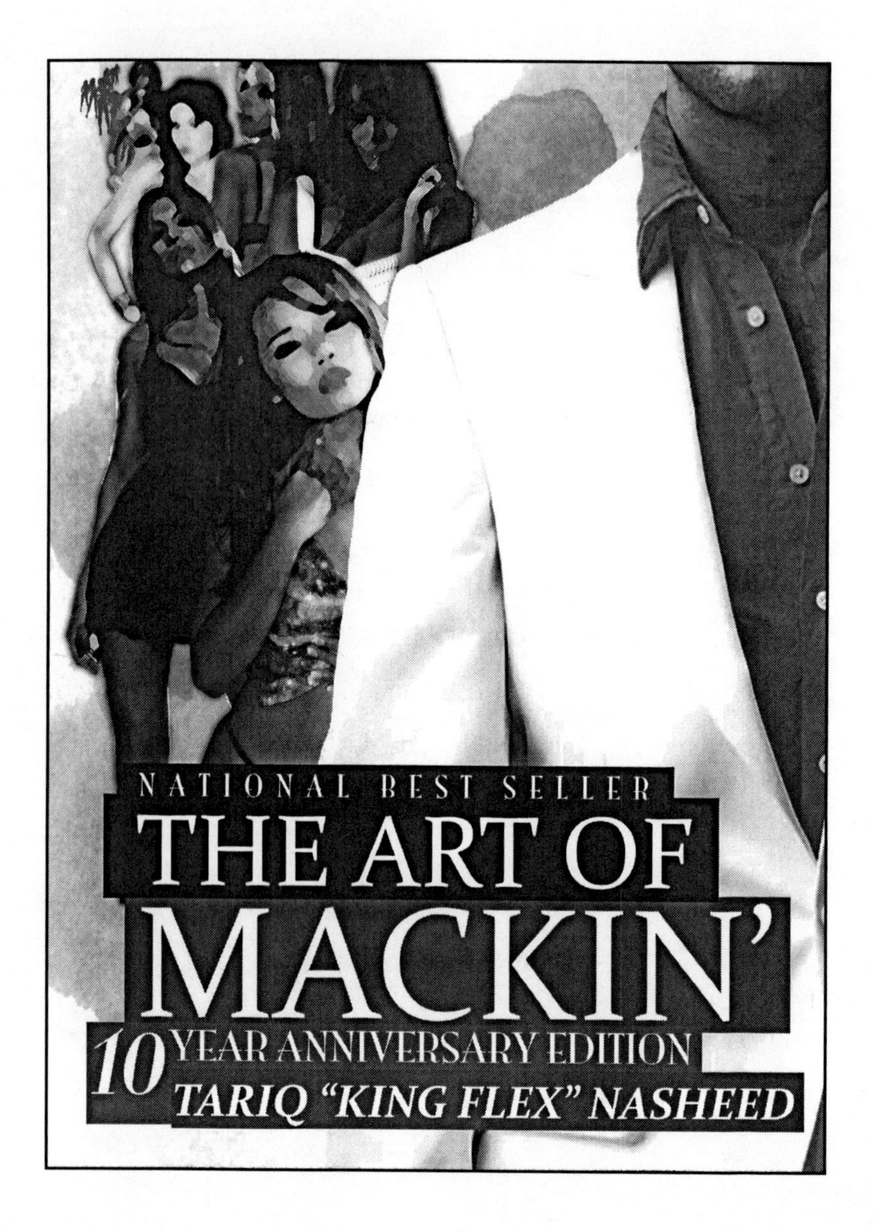
NATIONAL BEST SELLER
THE ART OF
MACKIN'
10 YEAR ANNIVERSARY EDITION
TARIQ "KING FLEX" NASHEED

OTHER BOOKS BY TARIQ "KING FLEX" NASHEED:

THE ART OF MACKIN'

252 pages

Publisher: G.D Publishing -King Flex Ent

"(This book) comes from the experiences of a seasoned veteran of the game" -- Kronick Magazine, March 2001

"A much needed book" -- Dave Shaftel,The Source Magazine

THE ART OF MACKIN' takes a fun, yet serious look at modern male/ female relationships from an urban point of view. The ART OF MACKIN' is the first "how to book" that teaches men how to actually become "players" and "macks."

THE MACK
WITHIN
The Holy Book of Game
Tariq "K-Flex" Nasheed

OTHER BOOKS BY TARIQ "KING FLEX" NASHEED:

THE MACK WITHIN

Paperback: 176 pages

Publisher: Riverhead Trade

The Art of Mackin' was the first book of rules for players-from overcoming fears of getting dissed to spotting a stank dead on. Now the expert on mackin' is back with the ultimate straight-up guide for every mack and mack-wannabe. Whether he's after ass or cash, trying to spit game at a Benz-driving Diamond Girl or a street-tough Copper Chick, or if he's just tired of being coochie-whipped, it's time to open up this book and unlock the time-tested secrets of the mack game.

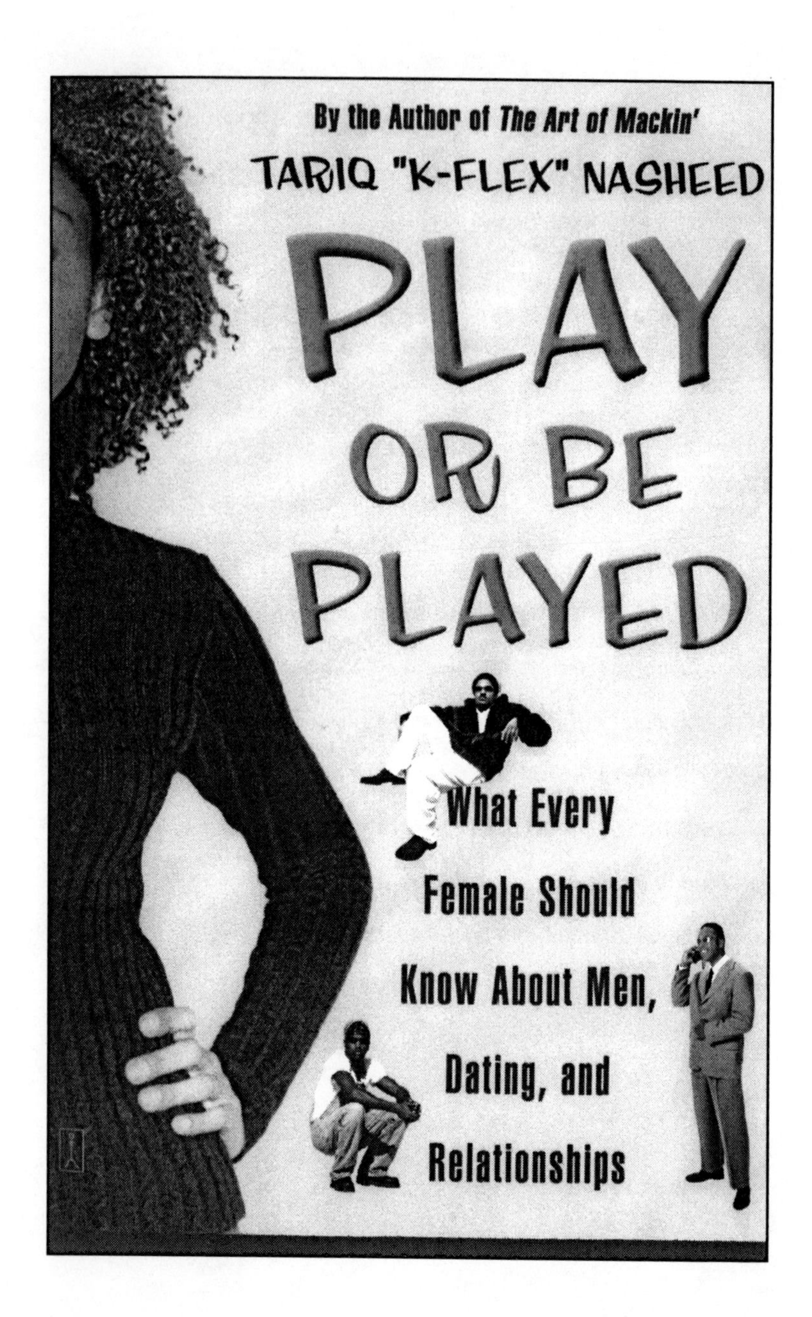
By the Author of The Art of Mackin'
TARIQ "K-FLEX" NASHEED
PLAY
OR BE
PLAYED
What Every
Female Should
Know About Men,
Dating, and
Relationships

OTHER BOOKS BY TARIQ "KING FLEX" NASHEED:

PLAY OR BE PLAYED

224 pages

Publisher: Fireside

Got Game?

It's a fact. Every woman needs game. Take Oprah, Jada Pinkett-Smith, and Beyoncé Knowles. All three of these women have the one intangible quality that every mack, male or female, must possess: they all have game. In other words, they have intelligence, hustle, and common sense that they apply to every aspect of their lives -- especially in their relationships.

Play or Be Played is an instruction manual for women who are tired of being played by men and who want to be players themselves. Though women may not want to play games, the truth is men often do. So women who hope to win in the game of love must first learn the rules. Bestselling author and true mack, Tariq "K-Flex" Nasheed shares:

ways to spot a scrub
what it takes to get with a baller
why men cheat
how men really judge women
the top three mistakes women make in relationships
Street-smart and straightforward, Play or Be Played will help you get with a king without being a hoochie, groupie, or a chickenhead.

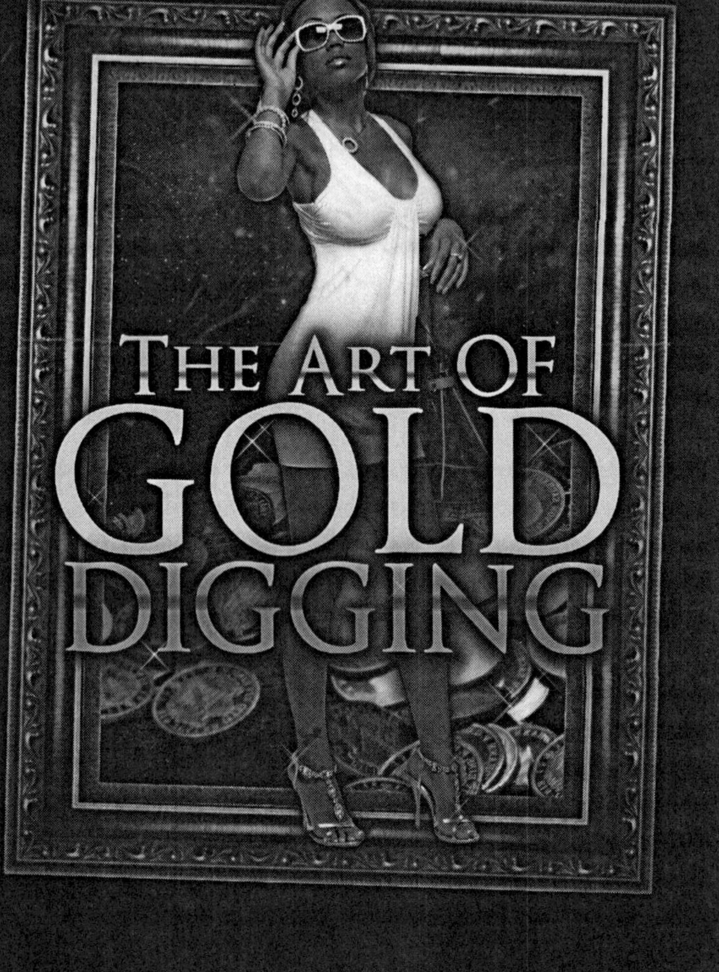
NEW YORK TIMES BEST SELLING AUTHOR
TARIQ "KING FLEX" NASHEED
THE ART OF
GOLD
DIGGING

OTHER BOOKS BY TARIQ "KING FLEX" NASHEED:

THE ART OF GOLD DIGGING

184 pages

Publisher. G.D Publishing-King Flex Ent.

The Art Of Gold Digging is the ultimate instructional guide to help women upgrade their game when it comes to dating. New York times best selling author Tariq King Flex Nasheed teaches women how and where to meet wealthy men and how to get these men to lavish them with gifts and riches.

MACK LESSONS

CPSIA information can be obtained at www.ICGtesting.com
Printed in the USA
LVOW08s2014281113

363147LV00001B/39/P